REFUGE UNDER HIS WINGS

OLUWAKEMI. O. OLA-OJO

Copyright © 2008 & 2009 Protokos Publishers

Refuge Under His Wings

Unless otherwise stated, all Scripture quotations are from the King James Version (KJV) of the Holy Bible.

Refuge Under His Wings
ISBN 978-0-9557898-0-9

Copyright © 2008 & 2009 by Oluwakemi O. Ola-Ojo
All rights belong exclusively to Protokos Publishers.

Published by Protokos Publishers
P. O. Box 48424, London, SE15 2YL

www.protokospublishers.com
info@ protokospublishers.com
+44 (0) 75 3483 1807

Cover design by Prex Nigeria Limited
prexng_2000@yahoo.com
prexadvert@hotmail.com

Book layout by Nestto Graphix

Author's photograph by Hill Stanton

Printed by Lightning Source, United Kingdom.

Printed in the United Kingdom. All rights reserved under International Copyright Law. Contents and or cover may not be reproduced in whole or in part in any form without the express written consent of the Publisher.

DEDICATION

This piece of writing is dedicated to all:

The past, present and future members of the Christian fellowship of Queen Elizabeth Hospital, (former Greenwich hospital) London who in spite of their scattered rotas still find time to come together and pray with and for other believers, the hospital authorities, staff and patients.

Who have suffered a great loss of anyone or anything dear to them.

Also importantly, it is dedicated to you my dear reader.

ACKNOWLEDGEMENT

Our God deserves all the glory and praise for making it possible for me to write this book. Forever, I will be indebted to Him.

I acknowledge with thanks, the overwhelming support of all the members of the Queen Elizabeth Hospital (QEH) Christian fellowship for the limitless and genuine love that I received in the years of my service there.

I am grateful to God for my family and friends whose understanding, support and cooperation have blessed my life and writing. Much thanks to my brother Oladapo for adding colour to this book.

I cannot but appreciate Mrs. Pat Roach and Dr Ekpo for making time to go through this book in spite of their busy schedule, for their useful comments, and for writing the foreword. Many thanks to Mrs. Bolanle Sogunro for editing this book and to all who found time to read and comment on the book, I say thank you for their invaluable comments and encouragement.

Finally, I thank the staff of Protokos Publishers and Prex Nigeria Limited for the excellent work they have done and for making my dream come true in publishing this book.

CONTENTS

	Dedication	3
	Aknowledgement	4
	Foreword	7
	Preface	9
1.	Don't miss it!	11
2.	Provoking God's favour	39
3.	Time to sing a new song	57
4.	Marriage and motherhood	81
5.	Epilogue	91
6.	Poems	95
	1. Death	
	2. God has another Plan	
	3. I will lift up my Eyes	
	4. There on the Rock	
	5. The more Difficult	
	6. Meeting God in Adversity	
	7. The Tides	
	8. The Unfailing Source	
7.	Opportunity to Become a Christian	107

FOREWORD

Pat Roach (*Senior Pastor, New Covenant Church, Wandsworth Branch, London. Great Britain*):
I feel so excited and honoured writing a foreword to this spiritually sound book. When I went through it and saw the dedication and commitment of the author, I was so pleased that I readily accepted the opportunity to write a foreword.

This book is a fine work of thoughtful reading and study from Oluwakemi O. Ola-Ojo. I love the presentation of facts in *Refuge under His Wings*. Many areas of Naomi's and Ruth's lives are covered in this book. I therefore recommend it to every Christian, married or single, as an aid to developing a Godly character of total dependence on the covenant keeping God.

Dr. E. B. Ekpo MD, FRCP (*Queen Elizabeth Hospital, Christian Fellowship, Woolwich, London. Great Britain*):
This is an exhaustive analysis of the Book of Ruth in the Bible. The inspiration came from the study of the book of Ruth in the Queen Elizabeth Hospital Fellowship Group. The author combines her deep Christian conviction and excellent knowledge of the Holy

Scriptures to produce a must read for every Christian, married or single.

The book is interspaced with beautifully written prayers, which enables the reader to pause, pray and meditate on the revelations received. The book is also loaded with poetry like 'Thy will be done oh Lord' for those who may be facing an uncertain future or on a cross road of decisions.

I recommend Refuge Under His Wings unreservedly to all who wish to study the Scriptures deeper and with a prayer that the Lord will use it to enrich the lives of all those who will read it.

PREFACE

It was sometime in 2000 or 2001, at the then Greenwich District Hospital, London, where Christian members of staff came together weekly, that we decided to study the book of Ruth during our Tuesday midday fellowship meetings. Over the weeks of reading and studying together, I took some notes.

Shortly after the study, Oladapo, one of my brothers, came visiting me for about a week and I decided to share with him some of the lessons I had learnt. Little did I realise that much more insight awaited me as both of us went through the same story together. God's steadfast love never ceases, His mercies never come to an end, they are new every morning, for great is His faithfulness to us all. The word of God is forever new, relevant, timely and purposeful.

The title of this book is taken from Ruth 2:12 and I have written the story so that you, as well as members of the fellowship who missed some of the meetings will be blessed.

Extensive portions from the Bible have been quoted from the book of Ruth. This will help the reader as he/she can easily follow the story if there is no Bible readily at hand. I have also provided space at the end of every chapter for writing your personal notes as you read. I pray that we all may be blessed as we read and meditate on this individually or in a group in Jesus' name.

CHAPTER 1
DON'T MISS IT!

Now it came to pass in the days when the judges ruled, that there was a famine in the land. And a certain man of Bethlehemjudah went to sojourn in the country of Moab, he, and his wife, and his two sons. And the name of the man was Elimelech, and the name of his wife Naomi, and the name of his two sons Mahlon and Chilion, Ephrathites of Bethlehem Judah. And they came into the country of Moab, and continued there.

And Elimelech Naomi's husband died; and she was left, and her two sons. And they took them wives of the women of Moab; the name of the one was Orpah, and the name of the other Ruth: and they dwelled there about ten years.

And Mahlon and Chilion died also both of them; and the woman was left of her two sons and her husband. Then she arose with her daughters in law, that she might return from the country of Moab: for she had heard in the country of Moab how that the LORD had visited his people in giving them bread.

Wherefore she went forth out of the place where she was, and her two daughters in law with her; and they went on the way to return unto the land of Judah.

And Naomi said unto her two daughters in law,

Go, return each to her mother's house: the LORD deal kindly with you, as ye have dealt with the dead, and with me.

The LORD grant you that ye may find rest, each of you in the house of her husband. Then she kissed them; and they lifted up their voice, and wept.

And they said unto her, Surely we will return with thee unto thy people.

And Naomi said, Turn again, my daughters: why will ye go with me? are there yet any more sons in my womb, that they may be your husbands?

Turn again, my daughters, go your way; for I am too old to have an husband. If I should say, I have hope, if I should have an husband also to night, and should also bear sons;

Would ye tarry for them till they were grown? would ye stay for them from having husbands? nay, my daughters; for it grieveth me much for your sakes that the hand of the LORD is gone out against me.

And they lifted up their voice, and wept again: and Orpah kissed her mother in law; but Ruth clave unto her.

And she said, Behold, thy sister in law is gone back unto her people, and unto her gods: return thou after thy sister in law. And Ruth said, Intreat me not to leave thee, or to return from following after thee: for whither thou goest, I will go; and where thou lodgest, I will lodge: thy people shall be my people, and thy God my God:

Where thou diest, will I die, and there will I be buried: the LORD do so to me, and more also, if ought but death part thee and me.

When she saw that she was steadfastly minded to go with her, then she left speaking unto her.

So they two went until they came to Bethlehem. And it came to pass, when they were come to Bethlehem, that all the city was moved about them, and they said, Is this Naomi?

And she said unto them, Call me not Naomi, call me Mara: for the Almighty hath dealt very bitterly with me.

I went out full and the LORD hath brought me home again empty: why then call ye me Naomi, seeing the LORD hath testified against me, and the Almighty hath afflicted me?

So Naomi returned, and Ruth the Moabitess, her daughter in law, with her, which returned out of the country of Moab: and they came to Bethlehem in the beginning of barley harvest. (Ruth 1:1-22)

This is the true story of a family whose historical background is dated to the time "in the days when the judges ruled." There was no calendar in those days as we now have it, so the exact date cannot be more specific. It was the period after the death of Joshua and the generation that witnessed the mighty delivering hand of God; before the time of the kings in Israel (Judges 2:8-19). Subsequent generations grew up who did not know the Lord or the work that He had done for Israel. If the children of Israel had followed God's commandment written in Deuteronomy 6:4-9, there would not have been any generation that did not know God.

Elimelech's generation may not have witnessed the mighty hand of God directly but they had enough history written down for them by Moses and Joshua to follow (Deuteronomy 31:22-30; Joshua 22-24). Like that generation in the book of Ruth, our generation today is so much blessed with the written history of the acts of God. Coupled with today's technological advancement, all this should normally draw us closer to God our maker not otherwise. The responsibility of keeping the next generation informed rests with us — true Christians.

The story begins with the information that due to famine, a man left Bethlehem with his wife and his two sons to live in another country called Moab. The Moabites were the descendants of Lot (Genesis 19:30-37). What caused the famine? God does not allow any nation to suffer famine except when that nation has sinned against Him. Famine is one of the ways that God uses to punish a nation that has turned against Him and His commandments. see Deuteronomy 28:15 – 24; (Leviticus 26:14-20; 2 Kings 6: 25-30). On the other hand, some people see famine as very natural but which ever way, countless lives are usually lost in famine due to hunger and starvation.

A time of national disaster such as famine is a time for national confession of sins, repentance and seeking the face of the Lord; not for running away. Too often, many blame their government or national leaders when there is famine instead of seeing it as a collective punishment for sin.

Evil prevails wherever Christians refuse to influence their government by prayers, or be an active part of the decision making in their land to effect Godly decisions. How many claim to be Christians in Church but are something else at home, at work or in the community? What of the 'once-a-week Christians'; those that are Christians only on Sundays? As salt they may have lost their taste and Christ-like influence; no longer relevant to the society or decision-making process. Some so-called Christians are worse than unbelievers in their relationships in the community.

We must stop blaming the government or our leaders. It is time to acknowledge our sins – individual and collective – before God for all have sinned and come short of the glory of God (Romans 3:23). If God were to mark iniquities not one of us could stand. Someone once said the events in a nation are the believer's report sheet. Where believers have failed to diligently play their roles in prayers of confession, intercession and supplications; have refused to actively participate in the running of the government of the day; have not openly confronted evil or are passive to ungodly decrees; have lived for themselves, their greed and not for God; have not brought up their children in the fear of the Lord or respect for authority, there is bound to be God's judgement in one form or the other. A genuine national repentance and turning away from sin unto God will always bring God's mercy and forgiveness:

If my people, which are called by my name, shall humble themselves, and pray, and seek my face, and turn from their wicked ways: then will I hear from heaven, and will forgive their sin, and will heal their land (2 Chronicles 7:14).

In the time of the Judges, the famine was real and Elimelech, like most fathers from Bethlehem (meaning house of bread), thought of what to do and where to go. With all good intent and purpose, Elimelech moved from Bethlehem in Judah to live in Moab, which he felt was a greener pasture, but sadly he did not consult God or get clearance from Him as that was not recorded in the Bible.

WHERE TO GO AND WHAT TO DO

Many like Elimelech have moved their families to a culture where they have now 'lost' their children to the new adopted culture. Children who are no longer respectful nor caring. Children who sometimes abandon the God of their parents for the 'new age thing' etc. Children who have now been lost to the system or does not want to identify with their rich roots or support their families especially their parents. Many options of where to go and what to do may be open to us in times of famine but we need to prayerfully consider each option. We must avoid reacting to events including national famine based on the physical circumstances around us, lest we move from God's land of promise to Sodom and Gomorrah, which from afar might look more promising than our homeland but in which awaits destruction and death.

You and I need to ask God where He would want us be, rather than apply head knowledge and limited human wisdom in our prevailing situation. The best place to be is God's place for us at that moment in time. God is still able to meet our needs, in spite of famine or national calamity, according to His riches in glory through Christ Jesus not through any other means.

There is a global famine of the word of God at present. Many people of this generation have deliberately migrated from the Lord to things such as New Age, hypnotism, mediums, stones/idol worship, etc.

Elimelech's name meant - Jehovah is my God, my Lord is king and his wife's name was Naomi which meant pleasantness (Ruth 1:2). They named their sons — Mahlon, meaning sick and Chilion, meaning pinning. Both names did not reflect this couple's belief in God.

What is in a name you might ask? A name, many times, carries the destiny and the characteristics of a person. There is a lot of power in the spoken word. It would seem that a person's destiny is locked in his or her name. Whatever you name your child and call him or her, will invariably affect the future of that child.

If you doubt that, see Isaac, meaning laughter (Genesis 21: 1- 6); Jacob, meaning cheat (Genesis 25: 26 – 27); Jabez, meaning sorrow/affliction (1 Chronicles 4:9 -10); Nabal, meaning folly (1 Samuel 25:25). Those who had negative names either died tragically like Nabal; had their names changed in order for their destiny to change like Jacob, or like Jabez, prayed intensely for a change.

In some cultures, like the *Yorubas* in Nigeria, a child is named according to the family belief; family status or circumstances surrounding the child's birth (see 1 Chronicles 4:9-10). Parents ought to be careful in choosing names for their children for as a man's name is so he is. Why call that child 'Junior' if you want him or her to exceed the parent's status in life? Parents ought to spend time seeking God's face before deciding their child's name. Giving a child a name without knowing its meaning can be dangerous to the child's future. Christian parents should also avoid just naming their child after a celebrity the meaning of whose name or even personal belief is unknown.

Others might give you another name based on a physical or medical condition or you might choose a nickname yourself. Whichever way you might have acquiredyour name, you need to re-evaluate that name especially if it is working against you or bringing you bad luck. You may even have to change it if necessary. Why name a child according to the prevailing circumstances of his or herconception or delivery especially if it is negative? Consider the destiny of the child instead.

Perhaps your name has haunted you like that of Jabez and there seems to be no breakthrough yet; do what Jabez did and receive a new and Godly destiny:

Jabez was more honorable than his brothers. His mother had named him Jabez, saying, "I gave birth to him in pain." Jabez cried out to the God of Israel, "Oh, that you would bless me and enlarge my territory!" Let your hand be with me, and keep me from harm so that I will be free from pain." And God granted his request. (1 Chronicles 4:9-10, NIV).

Jabez traced his bad luck in life to his name, which meant affliction or sorrow. He realised that only Jehovah God could break this yoke, he therefore prayed to God, giving Him specific requests namely, —

- ❑ That God will bless him (*the blessings of the Lord maketh rich and adds no sorrow to it* - Proverbs 10:22);

- ❑ Enlarge his territory i.e. remove him from all previously placed restrictions over his life, give him more opportunities, more blessings and promotion;

- ❑ That God's hand be with him (*If God be for you,*

no one can be against you – Romans 8:31. Christ in us is our only hope of glory) and

- ❏ That God should keep him from all hurt and harm. It is only in God that one is secured from all harm.

An enlarged coast will definitely require more protection for both the coast and the owner from the attacks of Satan. To be truly prosperous means having peace and security with our God-given wealth. No wonder the Psalmist said, *the Lord is my light and my salvation; whom shall I fear? the Lord is the stronghold of my life; of whom shall I be afraid?* (Psalm 27:1; see also Psalm 23, Psalm 46).

Praying like Jabez always works. In case your name like Jabez, has brought you nothing but pain, grief and sorrow, you may wish to pause and say one or both of these prayers:

Dear Lord God,

Thank You for giving me the chance to come to You now. I acknowledge my sins and confess them all to you including … (you may wish to mention as many of the sins you remember). I realise that by my ownworks, I cannot get to heaven or become Your child. I believe in Jesus Christ that He is the only Son of God, who came to die for my sins. I repent of my sins and with Your help will make a conscious effort not to go back to those sins. I ask You Father, to please forgive me of all my sins, cleanse me with the blood of Jesus and I invite Him to please come into my heart and be my Lord and Saviour from now on. Thank You Lord for granting me my request and for making me your child , a co-heir with Jesus Christ.

Thank You Lord as I am now born-again in Jesus name. Amen.

Dear Lord God,

I am grateful to You for the privilege of reading this literature and the ability to pray. Father as Your child, having been born-again and cleansed by the blood of Jesus Christ shed on the cross for my sins; I come before Your throne of grace, boldly at this time of my need. I realise that my name and/or the names that I have acquired – nicknames inclusive over the years have put me in many unfavourable, painful and sorrowful positions. I choose to forgive those who gave me these names and to forgive myself for acquiring such names. Father do please forgive my sins and in Your mercy, give me a new name like You did for Jacob, Abram and Sarai, and a new beginning of a purposeful, prosperous, pain free and protected life like You gave to Jabez in Jesus name. May there be a significant positive transformation in my life that You would bless me and make me a blessing from now on in Jesus name I pray with thanksgiving. Amen.

CONSEQUENCES OF WRONG DECISIONS

Elimelech's family moved to Moab and remained there (Ruth 1:2b). Moving away from the will of God is dangerous but remaining away from His will can be destructive if care is not taken (See also Genesis 13:8-13, 19: 1-29).

Soon Elimelech died, his sons got married and about ten years later, they also died without having any children, leaving behind them three hurting widows.

What Elimelech was avoiding by moving out of Judah was death but that still caught up with him and his sons abroad in the so-called 'greener pasture'. As in the case of Job, what Elimelech feared most happened to him (Job 3: 25).

There is a consequence for every decision or action that we take or don't take. For Elimelech's family that had no clearance from God before they moved, there was:

- ❏ Death of family members (verses 3-5)
- ❏ Lack/poverty (verses 7-8)
- ❏ Shame and sorrow (verses 13, 20-21)

Naomi now had no husband, sons or grandchildren to look after her. All she had left were her two daughters-in-law, Ruth and Orpah. In the midst of her sorrow, Naomi heard that the Lord had visited His own in Judah and had given them food. The Lord will not be forever angry with His people especially when they repent of their sins and return to Him.

Abundance of food in the land is a sign of God's forgiveness and blessings (Deuteronomy 28:1–14). God is love; though He hates sin, He loves the sinner. Although she was in another country, Naomi must have still kept in touch with home news. Nehemiah also did the same (Nehemiah 1:1-4). Are you a stranger in another man's land like Ruth or Nehemiah and still keeping abreast of your homeland news or have you, like the prodigal son, moved away from the Lord?

It is good to hear such brilliant news that there is now food at home again but what we do with the news we hear is more important. Remember Nehemiah who repented on behalf of his people and stood in the gap (Nehemiah 1:2-18) and Blind Bartimeaus who heard that Jesus was passing by and started shouting and pleading for mercy from Jesus Son of David (Mark 10:46-52).

'THE FARTHER AWAY YOU ARE FROM GOD, THE FARTHER YOU MAY BE FROM PROTECTION AND THE NEARER TO DESTRUCTION.'

Have you wandered away physically from your home like the prodigal son or runaway Hagar? Or have you spiritually packed up your faith in the living, risen Saviour and gone after other 'gods'? Be encouraged, this is the time and opportunity for you to return to God or to your home even as you read now: *For thus said the Lord God, the Holy One of Israel: In returning and rest you shall be saved: in quietness and trust shall be your strength* (Isaiah 30:15).

No one who comes to God will be cast away. However far you think you have wandered away from home and the Lord, He is able to save you, forgive you, cleanse and restore you (See 1 John 1: 8 – 9). Please pause and say either or both of these prayers:

Dear God,

I thank You that I am able to come to the end of myself and the beginning of Yourself. For far too long, I have lived and acted as not needing You Lord in many ways, but right now I realise that only in You do all people including me live, move and have their being. Lord God, I am a sinner and incapable of helping myself, I ask Jesus to come into my heart and live in my heart and be my Lord, Master and Saviour as from now on. I thank You Lord that my sins, though many, are forgiven by the blood of Your Son Jesus Christ and only in Him, have I been set free from all my sins and sicknesses. Holy Spirit, I thank You for introducing me to Jesus Christ my Saviour and Lord and to God my heavenly Father. According to Your word dear God, as I call on You, please hear me and save me. In Jesus name I have prayed with thanksgiving. Amen.

Dear Lord,

I acknowledge the fact that I have wandered away from home and my family in Christ. I now confess my sins including (you may wish to list your known sins here). I do this according to Your word in 1 John 1:7 -9 that says, 'the blood of Jesus Your Son cleanses me from all my sins. If I say that I have no sins, I deceive myself, and the truth is not in me, if I confess my sins, You are faithful and just to forgive me from my sins and cleanse me from my unrighteousness. Thank You for Your Son Jesus who died for my sins.

Thank You for the Holy Spirit who will help me not to return to those sins again. As I have confessed my sins, I thank You for honouring Your word and forgiving me. With Your help and in the light of Your forgiveness, I now consciously forgive myself and others who have used me and hurt me. I prayerfully put my hands in Yours, trusting You for a better, purposeful and fruitful future. In Jesus name I pray with thanksgiving. Holy Spirit I invite You into my heart to live in me from now in Jesus name. Amen.

AUDIT YOUR LIFE AND ACTIONS

There is a time for everything, including auditing your life and actions. Naomi must have carefully assessed the options of continuing to stay in Moab or a painful, sorrowful and empty return home. Even in her sorrow, she found time to face the reality of no husband, sons or grandchildren. Shameful as it was going to be, she was prepared to retrace her steps.

'BACK TO GOD, BACK TO GOOD
BACK TO GOD, BACK TO FAITH AND HOPE.
BACK TO GOD, BACK TO BLESSINGS.'

The love and acceptance available at home cannot be compared to the lack of fulfilment and hopelessness outside of God. Like the prodigal son, Naomi possibly realised that her destiny and blessings lay with her being in Judah under the canopy of the Almighty God (Luke 15:17-20). Naomi did not stop at the planning stage of returning home; she actually put her plans into action. Many have been robbed by the demon of procrastination. No one knows what the next minute would hold so we must redeem the time whenever we have the chance to do so . Please do not delay your accepting Jesus as your Lord and Saviour or delay rededicating your life to Him. God has not finished with you yet even though where you are now may seem like a 'dead end'.

Naomi set out with her two daughters-in-law to return to Judah. Both women — Ruth and Orpah — must have heard stories of the God of Israel, enough for them to want to leave their own gods, culture and family to follow their old mother-in-law to her country. They also must have had a good relationship with her so much as to willingly set out to follow her back to Judah, more so when there were no automobiles, trains or airplanes.

What is your relationship with your mother, father, brother or sister-in-law?

There is the true story of a young man and a lady in a relationship that they both hoped would blossom into marriage. In the course of conversation, the lady one day mentioned that she would not want to have a mother-in-law.

The young man's mother was very much alive at the time so his response was that when it will be time for the lady's children too to get married, their partners too would not want her as a mother-in-law! Their relationship never blossomed into marriage.

Do you see your in-laws as a blessing, a problem or a curse? So long as it depends on you, live at peace with others. It is not too late to be reconciled with your in-laws if you have been at loggerheads with them. As your ways please the Lord, He will make everyone, including your in-laws, to be at peace with you (see Proverbs 16:7).

Naomi did not take advantage of her daughters-in-laws. She objectively and openly addressed their future with her, and as such she gave both women the opportunity of returning to their families and getting married again. As you address your future, it is important that the future of those affected by your prevailing circumstances be prayerfully and carefully considered too.

Since no man can eat or drink for another person, no matter how much time we have spent witnessing to others, or speaking to them about something, there comes a time when we must allow them to make a conscious personal decision especially if it is one that would affect their future. A person's decision many times will determine his or her destiny.

Naomi did not blame any of her daughters-in-law for her loss. Rather, she blessed and appreciated them for their support of her and her dead sons. Even in her grief and darkest moments, she was still grateful to these women for their support and wished them rest and another happy married life. She kissed them and together all three of them wept. A case of family grief shared.

Naomi once again in her grief clarified the issues surrounding the repercussion of her daughters-in-law following her (verses 10-13). There is a Nigerian adage that sums this up by saying 'we do see even through our tears.'

Orpah took advantage of the offer and returned home. She possibly saw the physical not the spiritual outcome. She possibly felt it was better to live with the known than gamble with the unknown future in an unknown land with unknown people. How spiritually short sighted she was in this instance for we never heard of her anymore in the Scriptures. Unknowingly to her, she was being offered the chance to have her destiny changed for the best but she declined the offer. Some chances come only but once in life and unless we have the discernment of the Holy Spirit and trust in God, we may miss out.

Naomi had nothing to offer in terms of wealth and possession, she had no living son and she was poor. Ruth had nothing to gain from Naomi yet she chose to follow her. How will you and I classify the relationships we enter into — that from which we can make gains or profit or that to which we can contribute? God is interested in solid and purposeful life building. What is manifested in times of adversity is one's testimony.

After the second round of weeping, Orpah kissed

her mother-in-law and returned to her people, but Ruth clave to Naomi. Naomi again offered Ruth the chance of returning to Moab as Orpah had done but Ruth was determined to follow her mother-in-law.

We must equally be careful who we allow to follow us into our future. In the days of Gideon, when a call was made for soldiers to go to battle, many men turned up, but when the opportunity was given for the fearful to return home, twenty two thousand opted out (Judges 7:1-8)!

A wise person once said that most times, God would present our destiny changer in an unattractive offer or in a beggar's bag. Rebecca's destiny for instance was changed when she took up the offer to give Abraham's servant a drink and then watered even his camels too (Genesis 24: especially verses 10 – 21). Others had their destinies changed by the problems they solved – Joseph (Genesis 40:4-23, 41:14-46); Saul (1 Samuel 9-10:1); Daniel (Daniel 2:1-48); and Nehemiah (Nehemiah 1-2:6). Meeting a need can also translate into a change of destiny as in the case of the widow of Zarephath (1 Kings 17:7-6); the widow and her two sons (2 Kings 4:1-7); and the Shunamite woman (2 Kings 4: 8-17).

Sometimes the destiny change may come in form of a challenge to be faced on behalf of others e.g. David (1 Samuel 17;12-51); an intercession to be made on other people's behalf e.g Zechariah (Luke 1: 5-20) and Abigail on behalf of Nabal (1 Samuel 25:1-42).

Friend, do you know in what way your destiny is about to change? How short sighted is any one who applies only head knowledge and limited human wisdom to any situation that confronts him or her in life without consulting God. Many people are afraid of changes especially big ones, those that seem would disrupt their comfort zone such as moving away to live, work or fellowship somewhere else. If you are facing such a struggle, please pause, prayerfully read the following and then pray:

'THY WILL BE DONE OH LORD' (Luke 22: 42)

When like precious Joseph I am being abandoned
By those who are supposed to be very close to me Lord
Help me to keep doing all the good I know unto others
Looking forward to a breakthrough someday saying
Thy will be done oh Lord.

When at the war front against 'Goliath' I am prepared like David
And I am being offered all physical, man made weapons, Lord
Help me to remember that the arms of flesh will certainly fail
With boldness only in Your Word may I say
Thy will be done oh Lord.

When all hope has been lost like that of Jonah the Prophet
And in the submarine of discomfort, problems and uncertainty I find myself,
Remind me of Your promise that You will make all things work for good

And right there may I confidently say
Thy will be done oh Lord.

When I am seriously tempted to give up in my faith
In Your previous, precious revelations to me dear Lord
Remind me only of my past experiences and Your faithfulness
With a heart full of gratitude may I say
Thy will be done oh Lord.

When I am fed up with my job and my environment
And I feel rightly justified to do so dear Lord
Help me to remember how many souls You have blessed
In the process of my stay saying
Thy will be done oh Lord.

When my friends and family cannot understand me
And I cannot explain what I am doing and why Lord
Help me to remember that You are still leading me
Unto Your expected end and say
Thy will be done oh Lord.

When I am at the cross-road, unsure of what to do
And the vision seems to be tarrying on what next Lord
Help me to remember Your ever present presence with me
Communing with You and saying
Thy will be done oh Lord.

When I have to suffer for the sake of the precious gospel
And in the eyes of people I become a laughing stock
Remind me of Jesus Christ's experience on the cross
Boldly bearing the suffering saying
Thy will be done oh Lord.

When You are asking me Lord to do certain things
Things that are contrary to my own taste and nature
Remind me that Your ways are not my ways Lord
Obediently and willingly may I say
Thy will be done oh Lord.

When I have to give up things that are precious to me
Starting all over again in a new unknown environment
Missing all my good old friends, colleagues and loving neighbours
Thankful unto Thee may I say
Thy will be done oh Lord.

© **O. Ola-Ojo '90.**

Dear Lord,

I thank you for such an opportunity to read Your word, understand it and seek Your face. Thank You Lord that no one who comes to You, including myself, would be cast away. Lord I confess that I am struggling with some major steps and decisions. I need Your Holy Spirit and discernment in the following areas of my life at this time (please name them to the Lord). **Your** *word tells me that I should commit my ways unto You, trust in You and You will act. Your word equally says in Proverbs Chapter 3:5-6 that I should trust in the Lord with all mine heart; and lean not unto my own understanding. In all my ways I should acknowledge You, and You Lord shall direct my paths. Lord I confess that I am scared in the previously named areas of my life or in the decisions as previously named. Unless You, by the Holy Spirit,* *hold my hand, I will fall and fail. Thank you for granting me peace and clear directions in all that I have committed into Your hands today in Jesus name I pray with thanksgiving. Amen.*

DETERMINED IN SPITE OF CHALLENGES

We ought to avoid hasty decisions or commitments that we have not thought through. Ruth's decision to go with her mother-in-law meant a life long commitment to her, no matter the situation. From then on, Ruth was prepared to be loyal to her mother-in-law who had nothing to give her in return. How loyal are we Christians today prepared to be to God or His people? Ruth refused to be moved by Orpah's decision though they had a similar background in terms of culture and widowhood. How many today have missed the opportunities of becoming saved, or receiving various blessings including healing because of the popular opinion of others around them. They'll rather join the crowd than be seen to be alone in a Godly decision or action.

Salvation is personal. Today when you hear the voice of the Lord, do not harden your heart against Him. Friend, your decision in that matter or situation will determine your destiny. There were at least seven elements to the decision of Ruth to follow her mother-in-law back to Judah:

- ❏ A **new determination** – *Don't urge me to leave you or turn back from you.*
- ❏ A **new direction** – *Where you go, I will go….*
- ❏ A **new dependence,** coming under God's wings – *and where you stay I will stay.*
- ❏ A **new desire,** wanting only God's people – *Your people will be my people…*
- ❏ A **new devotion** – *and your God my God.*
- ❏ A **new dedication** – *Where you die I will die,*
- ❏ A **new destiny** – *and there I will be buried. May the Lord deal with me, be it ever so severely, if anything but death separates you and me* (NIV).

For the believer, nothing shall separate us from the love of Christ (Romans 8: 35- 39). When Naomi returned to Bethlehem with Ruth, the sadness within and on her face was very obvious. The whole city was moved by her plight whilst away from home but only one person was moved by the situation enough to bless them.

Dear friend, how you and I react to the poor, sick or less fortunate amongst us is very important. It is no good sympathising with the needy but refusing to bless them not only with prayers but also in practical ways. Our supportive faith must be put to action for 'faith without works is dead'. To us today, this may mean babysitting for that single mother once a week or more often so she could have some time to herself to pray and rest. It may mean cooking a meal or meals for the poor family in your church or neighbourhood or going to relieve that couple whose child is in the hospital so that they can have time to be alone or go home for a shower and a little rest. It could mean giving money or material goods to the widow or widower or sponsoring or taking into your home an orphan or someone who is homeless. The list is endless.

Whatever be the case, friend, be moved enough to empathise, give and support the unfortunate or needy around you. (see James 2:14-17)

BLAMING GOD

Four times in this first chapter, Naomi blamed God for her predicament, saying:

Things are far more bitter for me than for you, because the Lord himself has caused me to suffer (verse 13); for the Almighty has made life very bitter for me. (verse 20); I went away full, but the Lord has brought me home empty. (verse 21a); Why should you call me Naomi when the Lord has caused me to suffer and the Almighty has sent such tragedy?" (verse 21b)?

The blame game is still much alive as it was since the time Adam and Eve started it in Genesis 3. We know God does no evil, though He may permit it in His sovereign will. Naomi blamed God for her misfortune yet the Bible did not say that she or her husband consulted God before going over to Moab! Don't we still play the blame game too these days? Whom do we blame when things don't work out as planned or expected? Stop the blame game, my brother and sister! Be mature enough to confess your sins to God and trust Him to make your worst predicament work for your own good. (see Romans 8:28)

Naomi did not stop at blaming God; she decided to change her name to Mara, meaning bitterness. Obviously she had not learnt the importance of words and names. She based her new name, which could possibly stick to her until death upon a temporary bitter experience.

Would a change of name from pleasantness to bitterness solve the problem she was in at that time? No, it might even worsen her case for as one's name is so the person is likely going to be. How do you and I react under pressure?

Beloved, you and I need to watch our words The Bible says the words that we speak are spirit and life. Our words will create a positive or negative atmosphere around us; our words will attract either God's ministering angels or Satan's demons.

WE ARE TO ACT NOT REACT UNDER PRESSURE.

The fact that you and I are having some hard or trying times now does not mean it will be forever like this. The fact that you have failed or your much-wanted pregnancy has failed does not make you a failure. Weeping may endure for the night but joy comes in the morning. Please avoid making hasty decisions especially life long decisions based on temporary circumstances. Also, don't take decisions when you are physically weak, tired, hungry or sad lest you regret your actions later.

Naomi and Ruth's return to Bethlehem was in the beginning of the barley harvest. Best timing it turned out to be. Feeding was guaranteed for them especially since they could glean behind the reapers. The law of God through Moses in Deuteronomy 24:19-22 made provision for widows and strangers to glean after the reapers at harvest.

MY PERSONAL NOTES

CHAPTER 2

PROVOKING GOD'S FAVOUR

And Naomi had a kinsman of her husband's, a mighty man of wealth, of the family of Elimelech; and his name was Boaz.

And Ruth the Moabitess said unto Naomi, Let me now go to the field, and glean ears of corn after him in whose sight I shall find grace. And she said unto her, Go, my daughter.

And she went, and came, and gleaned in the field after the reapers: and her hap was to light on a part of the field belonging unto Boaz, who was of the kindred of Elimelech.

And, behold, Boaz came from Bethlehem, and said unto the reapers, The LORD be with you. And they answered him, The LORD bless thee.

Then said Boaz unto his servant that was set over the reapers, Whose damsel is this?

And the servant that was set over the reapers answered and said, It is the Moabitish damsel that came back with Naomi out of the country of Moab:

And she said, I pray you, let me glean and gather after the reapers among the sheaves: so she came, and hath continued even from the morning until now, that she tarried a little in the house.

Then said Boaz unto Ruth, Hearest thou not, my daughter? Go not to glean in another field, neither go from hence, but abide here fast by my maidens:

Let thine eyes be on the field that they do reap, and go thou after them: have I not charged the young men that they shall not touch thee? and when thou art athirst, go unto the vessels, and drink of that which the young men have drawn.

Then she fell on her face, and bowed herself to the ground, and said unto him, Why have I found grace in thine eyes, that thou shouldest take knowledge of me, seeing I am a stranger?

And Boaz answered and said unto her, It hath fully been shewed me, all that thou hast done unto thy mother in law since the death of thine husband: and how thou hast left thy father and thy mother, and the land of thy nativity, and art come unto a people which thou knewest not heretofore.

The LORD recompense thy work, and a full reward be given thee of the LORD God of Israel, under whose wings thou art come to trust.

Then she said, Let me find favor in thy sight, my Lord; for that thou hast comforted me, and for that thou hast spoken friendly unto thine handmaid, though I be not like unto one of thine handmaidens.

And Boaz said unto her, At mealtime come thou hither, and eat of the bread, and dip thy morsel in the vinegar. And she sat beside the reapers: and he reached her parched corn, and she did eat, and was sufficed, *and left. And when she was risen up to glean, Boaz commanded his young men, saying, Let her glean even among the sheaves, and reproach her not:*

And let fall also some of the handfuls of purpose for her, and leave them, that she may glean them, and rebuke her not.

So she gleaned in the field until even, and beat out that she had gleaned: and it was about an ephah of barley. And she took it up, and went into the city: and her mother in law saw what she had gleaned: and she brought forth, and gave to her that she had reserved after she was sufficed.

And her mother in law said unto her, Where hast thou gleaned to day? and where wroughtest thou? blessed be he that did take knowledge of thee. And she shewed her mother in law with whom she had wrought, and said, The man's name with whom I wrought to day is Boaz.

And Naomi said unto her daughter in law, Blessed be he of the LORD, who hath not left off his kindness to the living and to the dead. And Naomi said unto her, The man is near of kin unto us, one of our next kinsmen.

And Ruth the Moabitess said, He said unto me also, Thou shalt keep fast by my young men, until they have ended all my harvest.

And Naomi said unto Ruth her daughter in law, It is good, my daughter, that thou go out with his maidens, that they meet thee not in any other field.

> *So she kept fast by the maidens of Boaz to glean unto the end of barley harvest and of wheat harvest; and dwelt with her mother in* law. (Ruth 2:1-23)

Ruth adapted to the new culture and situation in Bethlehem, no more idol worshiping and so on, for she was confident that her mother-in-law would not lead her into destruction. In the same way, we ought to trust God now that we are born again knowing that He loves us too much to allow us to fall or fail so long as we walk with Him. We must learn to place our confidence in God for it will one day be rewarded.

Once Ruth was in Bethlehem, she faced the reality of no husband, immediate or distant relative, brother or father-in-law to take care of her. She faced the reality of the old age of her mother-in-law and the need to care for her so, she decided to go to work rather than wait for any form of charity. The weeping was over, it was now time for her to get on with life and make the best of it. She was bold to venture to work in a foreign land when she could have come up with several excuses not to go to work.

Ruth said to her mother-in-law, Let me go out into the fields to gather the leftover grain behind anyone who will let me do it.. Ruth had possibly learnt of the law that made provision for her feeding so long as she was willing to glean after the reapers. She was not a lazy woman; neither did she continue to wallow in her past life of sorrow, loss and misery. Someone has explained grace as an acronym for 'God's Riches at Christ's Expense'. Ruth went out in search of grace and she found it. Friend, when you are leaving home in the morning what do you go out expecting God to do for you? You should have an expectation for grace, favour, protection, supernatural provision, etc. (Proverbs 24:14)

Ruth decided to allow her mother-in-law to stay at home while she went to look for ways to feed both of them. It is the responsibility of children to look after their parents in their old age or when they are ill or cannot help themselves. The Bible says *he* [referring to both man and woman] *who does not provide for his family is worse than an infidel* (see 1Timothy 5:8).

Friend, when last did you bless your parents or parents-in-law? It does not matter what they have or have not done to us in times past, we are commissioned to bless them even in their old age. Of what use is an elaborate burial when your parent(s) literally starved to death? A preacher once said anyone who wants to have and maintain God's blessings ought to bless these three, namely:

- God
- His or her parents
- His or her pastor

We can bless God with our worship and love for Him, our songs and prayers, our time in His presence and for His people, in our substances given in tithes and offerings so that His priests might be fed and the kingdom work expands, in our giving to the poor, needy, widows, orphans etc.

Perhaps you doubt the need for you to bless your parents. From my personal experience and that of my friends, blessing your parents in word and deed is one of the easiest ways to find the favour of God upon your life. Bless them within your means. Give a specific amount of money to them regularly, weekly or monthly even if they are on state pension. Be there for them too in terms of spending meaningful time with them as often as possible and giving a helping hand with the chores e.g. helping with the laundry or shopping. As children tend to need the help and support of parents/adults in some things so, parents, especially later in life, do positively benefit from the kindness and generosity of their children.

Bless your Pastors with your prayers for them and their family. Encourage and appreciate them and as often as you can within your means; give gifts – it does not need to be that expensive – something that you know will be a blessing to them.

Ruth obtained her mother-in-law's permission before setting out. She knew she was a Moabite but trusted God to grant her grace through any field owner whom she could find. God's divine grace led Ruth in a divine direction to Boaz's farm and got her into the Boaz harvest. It is also grace that gets the sinner into the commonwealth of Christ. Read and meditate a while on this song :

> *Amazing grace! How sweet the sound*
> *That saved a wretch like me!*
> *I once was lost, but now am found;*
> *Was blind, but now I see.*
>
> *'Twas grace that taught my heart to fear,*
> *And grace my fears relieved;*
> *How precious did that grace appear*
> *The hour I first believed.*
>
> *Through many dangers, toils and snares,*
> *I have already come;*
> *'Tis grace hath brought me safe thus far,*
> *And grace will lead me home.*
>
> *The Lord has promised good to me,*
> *His Word my hope secures;*
> *He will my shield and portion be,*
> *As long as life endures.*
>
> *Yea, when this flesh and heart shall fail,*
> *And mortal life shall cease,*
> *I shall possess, within the veil,*
> *A life of joy and peace.*
>
> *The earth shall soon dissolve like snow,*
> *The sun forbear to shine;*
> *But God, Who called me here below,*
> *Shall be forever mine.*

When we've been there ten thousand years,
Bright shining as the sun,
We've no less days to sing God's praise
Than when we'd first begun.

Words: John Newton,
Olney Hymns (London: W. Oliver, 1779)
(MIDI, score). Source://cyberhymnal.org

Friend, how true that you and I need God's divine grace in whatever venture we embark on. Grace gives divine favour and can open the necessary doors to our destiny. However, we each have a part to play as the poem below will show.

GOD'S PROVISION - My Part

God has enough provision for all the people in the world who
will dare to call upon Him for help with their needs? In His
storehouse, there is abundance for despatch
But each one with a need has a part to play in receiving.

In the Garden of Eden, there was an abundance of food
Fruits, vegetables, fishes and all types of animal meat
But Adam and Eve had to choose what they wanted to eat
As well as go and get it for themselves whenever they wanted.

The manna and quails, God provided for the Israelites
Without failing for forty years on their way to the land of Canaan
Daily except the Sabbath they had to go 'collecting their meals'
In form of the manna flakes in the morning and quails in the evening.

The widow with her two sons were in great financial distress
Unknowingly to them the jar of oil was God's provision
They were to borrow as many pots and barrels from neighbours
By faith behind closed doors, poured the jar of oil into the vessels.

Another widow with her son were preparing for their very last meal
The famine was very severe with no hope for the next day
Elijah the prophet demanded that he be served first
And that was the beginning of a feeding programme for them.

For Peter and Jesus unable to pay their taxes when asked
Peter was instructed to go and fish in the sea
The first fish caught would have money in its mouth
Enough to pay for Jesus' and Peter's taxes as demanded.

God has promised to meet that need my brother, my sister
His part for providing for your needs He would fulfil
My part, your part in receiving would require total obedience
To God's instructions as He would graciously reveal.

My part, your part, my brother, my sister in meeting that need
Requires us to identify and accept that we indeed have a need
A need that only God can meet and He is willing to meet
Trusting in His abundant provision and obedience to His leading.

© Ola-Ojo 24/9/01 - 25/9/01

Ruth had the courage and willingness to go and glean in the fields where she knew no one, possibly something she had never done before in her own country. Unknowingly, Ruth found herself in the field belonging to Boaz, a relative of her late father-in-law. Faith in God will always bring divine appointment. She went out trusting God for favour and it's no wonder that she received it. We should go out each day asking God for His supernatural favour and expecting it. God's sovereign and saving grace led Ruth to wealthy Boaz's farm. Like the servant of Abraham, Ruth's testimony could be summarised as *I being in the way, the Lord led me* (see Genesis 24: 27).

Ruth did not take anything for granted as she took permission from the supervisor of the harvesting (see chapter 2:7). She obtained the necessary work permit before starting her gleaning. In that work that you are doing in a foreign land, do you have the required work permit? God expects believers to keep the law of the land wherever we find ourselves.

What does the foreigner have to contribute to our country? We must avoid stereotyping 'foreigners'. We need to reach out to the physical and spiritual refugees as we seek out God's purpose for sending them into our country. The harvest is indeed plentiful and it is harvest time, perhaps the Lord has brought some of these refugees to us so that they may find salvation within our land.

May God change our wrong attitude and help us so that we may let them go and glean on the fields for indeed it is harvest time. Many who have come to our countries have left their roots, family, friends and culture because of famine. This famine may be physical, material, social or even spiritual; they have risked so much to come to our land. Believe they each and all have something to contribute to our country even spiritually.

Many like Ruth are not seeking highly paid jobs but to glean after the reapers. They are looking for menial jobs to keep themselves and their dependants fed, clothed, housed and catered for. For the sake of the Kingdom, let's give them permission to do so within the law. Many are law abiding, not wanting to be illegal so, please let us accommodate them legally under the law.

Who would have envisaged that Jesus Christ would invariably come through Ruth the foreigner? Who knows what medical, engineering, technological, etc. breakthrough is lying within that poor foreigner/refugee? Who knows if the foreigner/refugee's intercessory prayers will move God to show us mercy instead of the punishments /wrath our sins could have brought? It just happened that while she was gleaning in the field, Boaz came from Bethlehem to visit his reapers. Boaz's initial greetings to his reapers were, *The Lord be with you.* What a relationship Boaz must have had with Jehovah to know that unless the Lord be with the reapers they laboured in vain (see Psalm 127:1).

The reapers' reply to him was *'The Lord bless you'*. We must be careful of what we sow into the life of others for it definitely would come back to us and definitely in multiple-fold.

Somehow too, Boaz was observant enough to notice

an unknown woman among his reapers. He asked his farm supervisor about her. Unlike Boaz, God knows all about you and me and needs no information about us. He is aware of all that we are going through and has adequately made provision ready for us if we would only seek Him, coming to Him just as we are. God's seeking grace made Boaz to ask about Ruth and talk to her first. God will use every means of communication, sometimes including trials and difficulties, to seek for us even in our sins.

Ruth didn't know that she was being watched. She was a woman of great strength and as she worked tirelessly among the workers, reports were being passed on to the boss and owner of the field. Her dedication and hard work did not go unnoticed. Beloved, it does not matter what others do at work, you and I are being watched first by the Almighty God, followed by a cloud of witnesses, colleagues and many more others than we can imagine. We ought to work as unto the Lord not as unto any man. For some people we are going to be the only Christians they will ever see. What testimony do we have at work? We should be witnesses at work.

Ruth found favour first with the supervisor and then with Boaz the field owner. Her on-the-job performance was quite impressive to Boaz who then spoke to her saying, *Let thine eyes be on the field that they do reap, and go thou after them: have I not charged the young men that they shall not touch thee? and when thou art athirst, go unto the vessels, and drink of that which the young men have drawn* (verse 9).

Boaz referred to Ruth as daughter and then gave her a permanent permit to work closely with his reapers. He reassured her of her safety from the men who might want to make a pass at her. Ruth was also permitted to re-fresh herself from the water which others had drawn. She did not take these permissions and favours for granted but in humility and gratitude she fell on her face at his feet bowing down and said to Boaz, "Why are you being so kind to me?" she asked. "I am only a foreigner." (see verse 10)?

Boaz, a Jew should not normally talk to this Moabite, who was a gentile, but God's divine grace made him do so. Boaz' response was very reassuring and thoughtful. He was willing to allow God to reward Ruth through him: *May the Lord, the God of Israel, under whose wings you have come to take refuge, reward you fully* (see verse 12).

Boaz in kindness also gave Ruth the permission to join his workers for a meal and water in the course of her work in his field (verse 12). That grace she found with Boaz was one that satisfied her physical hunger and thirst. Break or lunch time at work can be very lonely to new comers or strangers even now. Sharing meals with such people, pointing them in the right direction or even sitting with them at the dinning table could be reassuring and promote godly friendship.

God's grace:
- leads to the place of blessing
- gives supernatural wisdom and skill
- brings favour with those in authority
- gives security and protects from all forms of other people's abuse
- promotes one from a low estate to the commonwealth of God's family (Boaz called Ruth daughter not stranger or foreigner)
- provides for physical needs like water, food and shelter
- provides sustainable income (Boaz gave Ruth the permission to glean with his workers all through the harvest season.)

Ruth took the advantage of the invitation and obeyed by joining the others. Though she was doing a sort of voluntary work, she worked like any of the hired workers, returning to work after lunch. What do you do after your lunch? What is your habit like at work? Is it that of a lazy person or a committed hard worker or one who does eye service in the presence of the boss or clients?

When she stood up to glean, Boaz commanded his young men, saying, *"Let her glean even among the sheaves, and reproach her not: And let fall also some of the handfuls of purpose for her, and leave them, that she may glean them, and rebuke her not"* (see verses 15 and 16).

That grace gave her security and protection against any molestation from the young men in the field. If there is someone that we know who is going through some severe financial crisis or is unemployed due to no fault of theirs in our home group, church or neighbourhood, we ought to act like Boaz. Purposely leaving them money, food or clothing will just be in place in addition to inviting them for meals.

Ruth took home the reward of her work and the doggy bag (left over) from her lunch for her mother-in-law. What a caring daughter-in-law she continued to be. Naomi was obviously surprised at what Ruth brought back home and so inquired from her. When she learnt that it was Boaz, she had the discernment to acknowledge the sovereignty and provision of God.

There is need for us to be quick to appreciate God even in little things, as nothing just happens by itself. Every blessing that comes our way is from God who loves us and is in control of the universe. He demands, and is worthy of all our praise.

Ruth also informed her mother-in-law of the full-time gleaning opportunity in Boaz's field until the end of the harvest. The grace she received gave her a secured job throughout that year's harvest time. Naomi encouraged Ruth to remain in Boaz's field throughout the harvesting season. In obedience, Ruth worked alongside the women in Boaz's fields and gathered grain with them until the end of the barley harvest. Then she worked with them through the wheat harvest, too. But all the while she lived with her mother-in-law.

Though it was a sort of voluntary service, Ruth remained faithful, going there everyday and working very hard too. There are so many opportunities around us today. God who has allowed us to be alive at such a time like this has given us the privilege of harvesting souls for Him. It is sad to see many people quit their jobs when they are about to be promoted unknown to them. Unless God is leading you, friend, stop jumping around jobs.

Though things may look rough, no money today — stay there! Where God leads we must be willing to follow. Our geographical location has much to do with God's intended blessings for us. (see Genesis 12:1-3, Genesis 26:1-24, 1 Kings 17) Stay in the place of favour not in the place of labour. Be where you are celebrated not tolerated. God is able to provide streams in the desert, manna and quails in the wilderness of life and water from the rock. He can always be trusted.

MY PERSONAL NOTES

CHAPTER 3
TIME TO SING A NEW SONG

Then Naomi her mother in law said unto her, My daughter, shall I not seek rest for thee, that it may be well with thee? And now is not Boaz of our kindred, with whose maidens thou wast? Behold, he winnoweth barley to night in the threshing floor.

Wash thyself therefore, and anoint thee, and put thy raiment upon thee, and get thee down to the floor: but make not thyself known unto the man, until he shall have done eating and drinking.

And it shall be, when he lieth down, that thou shalt mark the place where he shall lie, and thou shalt go in, and uncover his feet, and lay thee down; and he will tell thee what thou shalt do.

And she said unto her, All that thou sayest unto me I will do. And she went down unto the floor, and did according to all that her mother in law bade her.

And when Boaz had eaten and drunk, and his heart was merry, he went to lie down at the end of the heap of corn: and she came softly, and uncovered his feet, and laid her down.

And it came to pass at midnight, that the man was afraid, and turned himself: and, behold, a woman lay at his feet. And he said, Who art thou? And she answered, I am Ruth thine handmaid: spread therefore thy skirt over thine handmaid; for thou art a near kinsman.

And he said, Blessed be thou of the LORD, my daughter: for thou hast shewed more kindness in the latter end than at the beginning, inasmuch as thou followedst not young men, whether poor or rich.

And now, my daughter, fear not; I will do to thee all that thou requirest: for all the city of my people doth know that thou art a virtuous woman.

And now it is true that I am thy near kinsman: howbeit there is a kinsman nearer than I.

Tarry this night, and it shall be in the morning, that if he will perform unto thee the part of a kinsman, well; let him do the kinsman's part: but if he will not do the part of a kinsman to thee, then will I do the part of a kinsman to thee, as the LORD liveth: lie down until the morning.

And she lay at his feet until the morning: and she rose up before one could know another. And he said, Let it not be known that a woman came into the floor.

Also he said, Bring the veil that thou hast upon thee, and hold it. And when she held it, he measured six measures of barley, and laid it on her: and she went into the city.

And when she came to her mother in law, she said, Who art thou, my daughter? And she told her all that the man had done to her.

And she said, These six measures of barley gave he

me; for he said to me, Go not empty unto thy mother in law. Then said she, Sit still, my daughter, until thou know how the matter will fall: for the man will not be in rest, until he have finished the thing this day. (Ruth 3:1-18)

Little did Ruth know that God was going to favour her because of her service and commitment to her mother-in-law. With time, Naomi began to think of Ruth and how to get her a husband. She was concerned about the total well being of her daughter-in-law and was thoughtful enough to realise her feminine needs even though the scriptures did not indicate Ruth voicing out this need. Food for Naomi and Ruth was secured but Naomi looked into the future for her daughter-in-law and wanted more for her in terms of a relationship and security for life.

In the same way, coming to God through Christ should be more than getting our daily needs met; it is an eternal relationship with Him that begins from here on earth. God knows our needs and He is able to connect us with the necessary destiny changer through whom our story will change for the best and we can sing a new song.

Most of us have a past that may not want to allow us to move on to a brighter and better future. God is able to give another opportunity in the same place or forthe same thing where we have once failed or fallen. Where once we have been mocked or laughed at, our

God can give us such a success that we will become celebrities. Most successful people in life had one or more times failed before.

Loss and failure are all part of life as well as gain and success. In His omnipotent mercy and love, God may give you another chance. What will you do when this opportunity comes? Once you have experienced that loss or failure and learned all the possible lessons, then please let go of the painful, unfruitful past and prayerfully embrace every God given new opportunity.

Dressing for where you are going is much more than a change of clothes or wardrobe, it may involve you putting an end to all the blames of the past, letting go of all previous hurts and bitterness, all unhealthy attitudes and behaviour, doing away with relationships that want to keep you in the past.

God will send people or events into your life that will lead you to a better future. For every Ruth there will be a Naomi. For every Moses there will be the priest of Midian, for every Saul of Tarsus there will be a Banabas, for every prodigal son there will be a loving father waiting.

Naomi was not selfish. Tough and painful as it may be for parents to loose their married son or daughter, after the time of mourning, please let the surviving son or daughter-in-law move on in life and do not hesitate to give the maximum support as Naomi did.

Naomi told Ruth what to do to change her marital

status and as Ruth carried out the plan, she got a husband indeed. Ruth was obedient and submissive to the authority over her — in this case, her mother-in-law. We ought to be obedient and submissive to every authority over us, no matter who it is, provided it does not contradict God's word. God does not bless disorder or disobedience. The steps Naomi told Ruth to take in order to find a husband are still very applicable today. They are contained in the first four verses of Ruth Chapter 3.

Even if you are not looking for a marriage partner, these principles still apply because every child of God is being prepared as a bride for Christ.

PRINCIPLE 1: LOCATE THE PERSON

Behold, he winnoweth barley to night in the threshing floor.

Finding a godly life partner can be very daunting for men and much more for women. God is able to send you a partner from your church, neighbourhood, workplace, in the bus, train etc. What is important is to be prepared at all times for no one can be sure of when and where the Lord will ordain for a man or woman to meet the much prayed for, wanted life partner. Many, especially men, have ended up marrying the person who helped them at a critical time in their life. As you await the husband or wife the Lord will lead to you or that you will be led to by God, begin to prepare yourself to be the best helpmate or husband that person could possibly have.

PRINCIPLE 2: CLEANLINESS

Wash thyself therefore

Cleanliness they say is next to Godliness. Basic hygiene is essential to good, acceptable presentation. Taking good care of one's body is important. Pay attention to your sleep and what you eat. Take regular baths/showers and guard against repulsive smells both from bad breath and sweat. How you look and much more how you comport yourself everywhere (talking and sitting inclusive especially for the woman) speak volumes about how clean you are as a person. Washing with soap and water is not only refreshing, but it is also good for the skin; it is the best way to having and maintaining good body smell.

The aim of Ruth's visit to Boaz was to seek for a relationship. Being created by God is very important, but we must also seek to have a relationship with our maker. God not only created Adam and Eve and placed them in the garden, He also visited them regularly (see Genesis 2 and 3). Sin made them loose this relationship but Jesus came to the world to restore it. Just as it is important for us to be physically clean before and during relationships, it is essential for us to be spiritually clean before we approach God with our requests As the bride

3 – TIME TO SING A NEW SONG

of Christ, one cannot come into the very presence of the most high God without first being washed in the blood of Jesus, just like the words of this song:

What can wash away my sin?
Nothing but the blood of Jesus;
What can make me whole again?
Nothing but the blood of Jesus.

Refrain

Oh! precious is the flow
That makes me white as snow;
No other fount I know,
Nothing but the blood of Jesus.

For my pardon, this I see,
Nothing but the blood of Jesus;
For my cleansing this my plea,
Nothing but the blood of Jesus.

Refrain

Nothing can for sin atone,
Nothing but the blood of Jesus;
Naught of good that I have done,
Nothing but the blood of Jesus.

Refrain

This is all my hope and peace,
Nothing but the blood of Jesus;
This is all my righteousness,
Nothing but the blood of Jesus.

Refrain

Now by this I'll overcome –
Nothing but the blood of Jesus,
Now by this I'll reach my home –
Nothing but the blood of Jesus.

Refrain

Glory! Glory! This I sing –
Nothing but the blood of Jesus,
All my praise for this I bring –
Nothing but the blood of Jesus.

Refrain

Words & Music: Robert Lowry, in Gospel Music, by Howard Doane and Robert Lowry (New York: Biglow & Main, 1876) (MIDI, score). Source://cyberhymnal.org

PRINCIPLE 3: PERFUME YOURSELF

... and anoint thee,

In the time of Esther the Queen, so much importance was placed on preparing to meet the king (Esther 2:8-12). This included anointing the woman with loads of oils and perfume for a year and so it remains in some cultures today. The Bible says it is by the anointing of the Holy Spirit that the yoke shall be broken.

Men in particular tend to be influenced by what they see and smell. Under normal circumstances, a person who is clean and who possibly is wearing a good perfume will physically attract others. The Christian life is meant to be like a fragrance, sweet perfume both to man and to God. As we yield every compartment of our lives to Christ through the Holy Spirit, we will draw more people to us who in turn can be led to Jesus Christ.

PRINCIPLE 4: DRESS WELL

... and put thy raiment upon thee,

This means dress well, be presentable and attractive to the man. Ruth was instructed to dress for where she was aiming for, not for the situation of widowhood in which she had been living for sometime. Boaz was a rich man and I wonder if a widow in tattered clothes would appeal to him. Woman, be aware that there is a demon that I refer to as the demon of the first impression. It has been in existence since the Bible times. See I Samuel 17: 17 and 33. When Saul saw David on the battlefield, not only did David look so young, he was also dressed as a shepherd not as a soldier or warrior, so the natural tendency was for Saul to look down on him. It took David some time and effort to convince King Saul that he was capable of killing Goliath. When he was finally convinced, Saul felt David's dressing did not match the occasion and so offered him his own military wear.

Another example is that of Esther's victory in the beauty contest. There was only one chance to be chosen as the queen from among many virgins. Esther was not the first virgin to be introduced to the king but she was the only one chosen to be queen. Why? I believe that it was God-ordained but at the same time, she was obedient to her uncle/adopted father and the Eunuch.

All the virgins were given the same food and body treatment but Esther excelled. Why? Esther was the only virgin who sought for the Eunuch's counsel on what to wear for her time with the king. The Eunuch must have known what would appeal to the king most and so advised Esther accordingly. Esther took the advice, she was crowned the new Queen instead of Vashti and there was no other need for another virgin. Often times there is no second chance to make the first impression.

Daughter of Zion, child of God, you need to start dressing for where you are going not where you are now. Take counsel from experienced godly people. Our inner appearance matters more to God than our outer appearance for while men look at the outward appearance, God looks at man's heart. At the same time we must avoid being deceived that being a Christian means lacking in taste and style — just accepting anyone or anything. Many have ruined their marriages andrelationships because of carelessness in this area. Dressing within our means is important but more so having clean clothes on; wearing what will enhance our God given beauty without undue body exposure. Guess what? The Holy Spirit is able to lead you to what to wear or not to wear every time you ask Him and He gets it right all the time much more better than the 'weather man/woman'. Once our character is pure and clean it becomes easier to radiate the beauty of Christ.

PRINCIPLE 5: BE PRESENT, BUT DISCREET

... and get thee down to the floor: but make not thyself known unto the man, ...

Be where the man is but keep away from him. There is a time to talk and there is a time to keep silent. It is better to be noticed and wanted than to put yourself forward and be rejected. My mother used to say that it is better to marry someone who loves you than someone you love but who does not love you. In other words, be with people who will appreciate and celebrate you than with those who can barely tolerate you.

PRINCIPLE 6: MAKE SURE THE MAN IS EATEN AND IS FULL

... until he shall have done eating and drinking...

As the saying goes, a hungry man is an angry man. Most men cannot play with their food or be interested in anyone when they are hungry. A story was once told of a bachelor who needed to choose between two likely Christian ladies to marry. So, he set up this flint test. He asked that the Lord would help him to know who among these ladies God would want him to marry.. He and his firend would visit both ladies and the lady that offered to feed them both without their asking for food should be God's choice for him. Truly, one of the sisters willingly offered to feed them and did feed them but the other did not offer them any food.

Correct timing is equally important for any serious discussion. Queen Esther did not try to beg for the lives of her people until the king's tummy was full (see Esther 7:1-6).

PRINCIPLE 7: PRESENT YOURSELF TO HIM AS GOD LEADS

... *thou shalt mark the place where he shall lie*, ...
Ruth was to present herself after Boaz had eaten and rested. This is the only account I am aware of, where the lady was asked to tactically woo the man. In many cultures it is otherwise but who can understand our God? His ways are not our ways neither are His thoughts our thoughts. Difficult as it was for Ruth and maybe for some of us, when God tells us to do certain things, our motto should be 'where and when He leads me I will follow.'

Ruth acted on her mother-in-law's instructions without any procrastination, complaint or compromise. She did not limit her obedience to only what she was comfortable with. It is unfortunate that many have lost their God-sent revelations when they procrastinated, complained or compromised.

3 – TIME TO SING A NEW SONG

PRINCIPLE 8: LIE AT HIS FEET, NOT BY HIS SIDE

... and thou shalt go in, and uncover his feet, and lay thee down; ...

Ruth lay down at Boaz's feet not by his side for she was not his wife by then. She did not wake Boaz up but patiently allowed him to discover her. She did not try to uncover herself to him for a one night stand; she kept her emotions and desires well under control. Much as she needed a man, a husband to love her intimately, Ruth was not going to soil her marriage bed or make herself cheap. How sad to see and hear of many women who in the light of going to seek for help, counselling inclusive, have seduced or have been seduced by married men and ministers of God to commit adultery with them, thereby causing such men to fall and fail. When all that needs to be done is done sister, do not parade yourself beside your potential husband or try to 'wake' him up. Let him find you out for himself.

PRINCIPLE 9: LET HIM FIND YOU OUT, DON'T TALK

... and he will tell thee what thou shalt do...

Ruth did not talk initially; she waited till Boaz noticed her. Around midnight, Boaz suddenly woke up and turned over. He was surprised to find a woman lying at his feet! "Who are you?" he demanded. ?" I am your servant Ruth," she replied. "Spread the corner of your covering over me, for you are my family redeemer." (verses 8 and 9).

In humility, Ruth referred to herself as servant. Now that she had been noticed and spoken to, it was time to talk and make a request of Boaz. She did just that in very few words without assuming the man ought to know or figure out why she must have been there at such a time as that. There is a time for everything says Ecclesiastes 3:1. In the presence of God our only Redeemer and Saviour we ought to cultivate the habit of talking especially in line with Philippians 4:6 – making our request known unto Him with thanksgiving. God knows all but He still wants us to ask in our own words. Salvation comes with a belief in our heart and our open confession (Romans 10:9).

Ruth asked for protection and security from Boaz. As we humble ourselves before God, we are allowed to ask for same. Only God can adequately cover anyone from shame, poverty, loneliness, sickness and pestilence, barrenness and all the ills of this world. He is the one that we ought to call upon in our times of need and distress. He is better than the mother hen or mother eagle.

Let us consider the reply Boaz gave Ruth:

The Lord bless you! This shows how truly loyal you are to your family. You could have looked for a younger man, either rich or poor, but you didn't. Don't worry, I'll do what you have asked. You are respected by everyone in town. It is true that I am one of the relatives who is supposed to take care of you, but there is someone who is an even closer relative. Stay here until morning, then I will find out if he is willing to look after you. If he isn't, I promise by the living God to do it myself. Now go back to sleep until morning. (Ruth 3:10-13, Contemporary English Version)

Boaz in his kindness did not scream at Ruth, rather he gently reassured her and once again, Ruth found favour with him. Boaz was impressed at being asked to inherit Ruth even though she could have opted for a younger man than himself. Indeed, Boaz was quick to acknowledge that there was another closer relative and did not take any advantage of Ruth nor molest her. Boaz was a man of integrity. He was discreet about Ruth's night out at the threshing floor and from the harvested grain, he blessed her with six measures of barley (Ruth 3:14-16).

Everyone including Boaz had noticed Ruth's noble character.

Character is not something that is built overnight neither can it be stolen from anyone. Someone once referred to character as a life long process, better than charisma. It is like a teabag whose brew is best seen in hot water, that is, during difficult times. Ruth returned home and informed her mother-in-law of her experience showing her the gift of barley. Ruth's obedience gave her success in this seemingly delicate matter. Life is very delicate, but our obedience to God's laws, those in authority, and the leading of the Holy Spirit is our sure way to success.

Naomi was confident of Boaz's ability to sort the matter out without any delay, for she said, "Just be patient, my daughter, until we hear what happens. The man won't rest until he has followed through on this. He will settle it today" (verse 18). God will always see that we are properly sorted out in that which we have made request of Him. God is not slow as many would want to think, neither is He slack in any of His promises towards us. He is always working on our behalf; He never sleeps, or slumbers neither does He go on holidays. In His time, He makes all things beautiful. Delay is not denial.

There was a divine stir in the heart of Boaz with regard to inheriting Ruth. What a testimony for any child of God to be so desired! Let me ask the single lady trusting God for a partner this question:

WHO IS YOUR IDEAL MAN?

Are you a Christian sister wanting to be married?
Perhaps, for so long you have been seeking the Lord's face
Perhaps you have not even been able to pray about this
Perhaps you need to be specific in your prayer requests
May I ask you dear sister, who is your ideal man?

Ask, it shall be given unto you. Seek, you shall find
Knock, and it shall be opened unto you says God

*And in asking, seeking and knocking, be specific
Even in this matter of getting married to your ideal man.*

*Many have chosen their man out of physical qualities
Many have based their choice on material capabilities
Many have been decieved by the demon of first impression
Many have been lured by family influence and affluence.*

*Do not be unequally yoked, God says to the single ones
The cost for such relationship could be too much to bear
The love is soon outlived for it has no solid roots to grow
The honeymoon is relatively short with severe aftermath.*

*Who is your ideal man dear sister, I ask again?
You need to give it a careful and prayerful thought
Good as it is to define his physical attributes
It is more important not to forget the spiritual qualities.*

*No two people are one hundred percent alike
Even identical twins, each still is different from the other
That's why you need to be specific in your request to God
Then you can be sure when God brings your ideal man.*

*Is he like Aaron, the excellent spokesman and assistant?
The priest of God who interceded on behalf of the people?*

*Is your ideal man like Abraham, the man of faith?
A friend of God and a daring intercessor?*

*Is he like Aquila, the professional tent maker?
Who opened his home for outreach and Paul's ministry?*

*Is he like Barak, the great army commander in his time?
The man who delivered Israel from Jabin, their oppressor?*

Is he like prosperous, thoughtful Boaz, the wise farmer?
Who was always blessing his workers and foreigners?

Is he like Caleb, the good reporter and wonderful warrior?
The man who waxed strong enough to conquer the land
At age eighty like when he was forty years old?

Is he like Daniel, the faultless administrator?
Who sought God all through his life even in the lion's den?

Is he like David, the man after God's own heart?
The poet, musician, warrior and successful king of Israel?

Is he like Enoch, who walked with God all through life?
That he was spared physical death for God took him?

Is he like caring, well-respected and intelligent Gamaliel?
His opinion within the council was unquestioned?

Is he like Gideon, the valiant warrior of God?
Who had peace first with God and then with his people
Who tested God twice with the fleece and was anointed?

Is he like forgiving prophet Hosea, who despite all odds?
Continuously redeemed his prostitute wife from her lovers?

Is he like Isaac, the meditating loner in the field?
The farmer who sought the Lord concerning his wife?

Is he like Jabez, who though was named sorrow?
Changed his destiny with prayers and excelled

Is he like Jacob, who wrestled with God and won?
The great cook, home lover, anointed and skillful shepherd?

Is he like Job, who in spite of the great loss

*Of his wealth, children, his health and Satan's trials,
Refused to curse God or sin proclaiming,
'I know my Redeemer lives'?*

*Is he like compassionate, caring and cheerful Joseph?
Forgiving, a man of great wisdom and administration*

*Is he like generous Jonathan and humble covenant-keeper?
He kept David away from his father's wicked plans,
He willingly relinquished his kingship right to David?*

*Is he like the young, strong and courageous Joshua?
A leader and an achiever, who dared to believe in God
Getting the people into the Promised Land?*

*Is he like Moses, the meekest man on earth?
The humble leader who stood in the gap several times
The teacher and one who spoke with God face to face?*

*Is he like stupendously rich but un-thoughtful Nabal
Who exposed his household to avoidable destruction?*

*Is he like Nathan, the wise and bold prophet of God?
Who dared to confront David about his sins
He pronounced God's judgments fearlessly?*

*Is he like Nichodemus, the profound scholar and teacher
Who humbly sought Jesus for salvation late in the night?*

*Is he like Noah, the only righteous man in his time?
Who warned the world as he built the ark for many years?*

*Is he like Samson, full of power and anointed of God?
Who avenged Israel's oppressors many times
And killed at his death more than when he was alive?*

Is he like Samuel, the anointed, respected prophet of God?
Who though very young heard Lord in the temple at night
And all through his life anointed kings for Israel?

Is he like Shadrach, Meshach or Abednego?
Men who would rather die serving God than bow to idols?

Is he like Simon Peter, the professional fisherman?
The bold leader of the disciples after Pentecost
Who after one sermon had three thousand converts?

Is he like Solomon, loved by God even before his birth?
The wisest, richest man, great composer and temple builder?

Is he like disciplined, committed, God-fearing Uriah
Who loved God and fought for his nation
Though killed through David's wicked's plot.

As you seek the Lord's face concerning a husband
You may need to spend time too, sister, in the scriptures
For the spiritual description of your ideal man.
© **Ola-Ojo '95**

By the same token, brother, may I ask you this question?

AND WHO IS YOUR IDEAL WOMAN?

A man who finds a good wife finds favour from the Lord
Amongst many women within and outside the Church

How do you go about choosing a wife my brother?
Charm is deceptive and beauty is fleeting

*But a woman who fears and honours the Lord
Is to be praised and rewarded.*

*Many men's lives have been enhanced or otherwise
Simply by their choice of marriage partner
Whilst some are being blessed, others are being destroyed.*

*The task of choosing a wife, beloved, is compounded today
Within our society of fast life and instant relationships
Internet datelines and many ungodly exposures.*

*Choosing a wife my brother needn't cause you fear
If you will humbly set time aside to seek God's face
Asking God for who your ideal woman is?*

*Is she like beautiful, thoughtful, wise, generous Abigail?
Though married to a fool, wisely interceded for her family?*

*Is she like Deborah; mother, wife, prophetess, and judge
Who bravely escorted and spurred army generals to war?*

*Is your ideal woman like Delilah?
Who throws a tantrum to find the source of your strength?
Yet conniving with the enemy to destroy her own man?*

*Is she like Elizabeth, who remained dedicated to the Lord?
Who though barren, yet faithful, became a mother in old age?*

*Is she like Eve, the suitable helpmate for Adam?
Who, decieved by the devil ate the God-forbidden fruit?*

*Is she like Gomer, Hosea's wife, the prostitute?
Who, though married, was unfaithful, seeking other men
And had to be redeemed often by her husband?*

Is she like Hagar, the slave and victim of circumstances?
Though she bore Abraham's heir was sent away for pride,
But sought the Lord and heard Him in her trying times?

Is your ideal woman like simple Hilda
A prophetess that heard from God about her country?

Is she like the orphaned, beautiful and obedient Esther?
In wisdom took wise counsel and become the chosen queen
She prayerfully put her life on the line to save her race
She approached the king with dginity and exposed her enemy.

Is she like Leah who, though not so beautiful, was fruitful
She lived to support their husband after her sister's death?

Is she like Lydia, the believer and famous seller of purple?
Though out on business attended fellowship on a Sabbath.
Was baptised with her family and also hosted the apostles?

Is she like Mary or Martha, sisters of Lazarus?
Who loved him so much and sent for Jesus when he was ill
Who listened to Jesus and hosted Him often in their home?

Is she like caring Miriam who watched over baby Moses?
The older sister who got him the best and suitable nurse
And later became the prophetess and singer?

Is she like Priscilla, the hospitable, welcoming tent maker?
Who always opened her home to Paul and other believers?

Is she like the beautiful but striving Rachel the shepherdess
Who for the love for her husband stole her father's idols?

Is she like Rebecca, who was so hospitable that

3 – TIME TO SING A NEW SONG

She gave watered the camel of Abraham's servant?
Who later comforted Isaac when his mother died
And prayed to God when pregnant with twins?

Is she like kind Ruth who would accept your God as hers?
Supporting your family with all her abilities and her life?

Is she like Sarah, the blessed mother of all nations?
Whose barrenness God turned into laughter in her old age?

Is she like young, virgin Mary who loved God so much?
She yielded to God's at the risk of loosing her fiancée?

Charm can be deceptive; beauty can be vain, dear bother
But a woman who fears the Lord is to be adored and praised.
Place your desire for the ideal woman before the Lord
Trust His guidance, timing amd way to this woman.
For he who finds a good wife finds favour from the Lord.
© Ola-Ojo 29.09.98 * Proverbs 31:30, Genesis 2:18-25

MY PERSONAL NOTES

CHAPTER 4
MARRIAGE & MOTHERHOOD

Then went Boaz up to the gate, and sat him down there: and, behold, the kinsman of whom Boaz spake came by; unto whom he said, Ho, such a one! turn aside, sit down here. And he turned aside, and sat down.

And he took ten men of the elders of the city, and said, Sit ye down here. And they sat down. And he said unto the kinsman, Naomi, that is come again out of the country of Moab, selleth a parcel of land, which was our brother Elimelech's:

And I thought to advertise thee, saying, Buy it before the inhabitants, and before the elders of my people. If thou wilt redeem it, redeem it: but if thou wilt not redeem it, then tell me, that I may know: for there is none to redeem it beside thee; and I am after thee. And he said, I will redeem it.

Then said Boaz, What day thou buyest the field of the hand of Naomi, thou must buy it also of Ruth the Moabitess, the wife of the dead, to raise up the name of the dead upon his inheritance.

And the kinsman said, I cannot redeem it for myself, lest I mar mine own inheritance: redeem thou my right to thyself; for I cannot redeem it.

Now this was the manner in former time in Israel concerning redeeming and concerning changing, for to confirm all things; a man plucked off his shoe, and gave it to his neighbor: and this was a testimony in Israel.

Therefore the kinsman said unto Boaz, Buy it for thee. So he drew off his shoe.

And Boaz said unto the elders, and unto all the people, Ye are witnesses this day, that I have bought all that was Elimelech's, and all that was Chilion's and Mahlon's, of the hand of Naomi.

Moreover Ruth the Moabitess, the wife of Mahlon, have I purchased to be my wife, to raise up the name of the dead upon his inheritance, that the name of the dead be not cut off from among his brethren, and from the gate of his place: ye are witnesses this day.

And all the people that were in the gate, and the elders, said, We are witnesses. The LORD make the woman that is come into thine house like Rachel and like Leah, which two did build the house of Israel: and do thou worthily in Ephratah, and be famous in Bethlehem:

And let thy house be like the house of Pharez, whom Tamar bare unto Judah, of the seed which the LORD shall give thee of this young woman.

So Boaz took Ruth, and she was his wife: and when he went in unto her, the LORD gave her conception, and she bare a son. And the women said unto Naomi, Blessed be the LORD, which hath not left thee this

4 – MARRIAGE AND MOTHERHOOD

day without a kinsman, that his name may be famous in Israel.

And he shall be unto thee a restorer of thy life, and a nourisher of thine old age: for thy daughter in law, which loveth thee, which is better to thee than seven sons, hath born him. And Naomi took the child, and laid it in her bosom, and became nurse unto it.

And the women her neighbors gave it a name, saying, There is a son born to Naomi; and they called his name Obed: he is the father of Jesse, the father of David.

Now these are the generations of Pharez: Pharez begat Hezron, And Hezron begat Ram, and Ram begat Amminadab, And Amminadab begat Nahshon, and Nahshon begat Salmon, And Salmon begat Boaz, and Boaz begat Obed, And Obed begat Jesse, and Jesse begat David. (Ruth 4:1-22)

The very next day after Boaz found Ruth lying at his feet, he kept his promise to her for, he approached the closer relative at the city gate, the usual place to discuss business in those days. Being a fair man, Boaz ensured that there were ten (number for government) other city elders at the time of discussion with the closer relative. He informed the closer relative of the land and inheritance of the late Elimelech.

Boaz was not greedy as he gave this relative the right to choose first while making it clear as well that if that relative was not interested, he would be (see Ruth 4:1-4). The closer relative without much thought agreed to buy the land but when informed of having to also marry Ruth according to the law of Moses, this relative backed out.

Boaz kept his promise again in the presence of the people by a public declaration: *Then Boaz said to the leaders and to the crowd standing around, "You are witnesses that today I have bought from Naomi all the property of Elimelech, Kilion, and Mahlon. And with the land I have acquired Ruth, the Moabite widow of Mahlon, to be my wife. This way she can have a son to carry on the family name of her dead husband and to inherit the family property here in his hometown. You are all witnesses today"* (Ruth 4:9-10, NLT).

It was now time for Boaz to publicly accept Ruth as his. He was not ashamed of her origin, past life or present condition but accepted her just as she was to give her a better future. When we confess Jesus as our Lord and Saviour privately, He openly and publicly affirms us as His, never again for us to live in the guilt, shame, sorrow, pain or loss of the past but to a glorious and fruitful relationship with Him.

Boaz was more concerned about fulfilling God's law than with being bothered about what he might loose by marrying Ruth. The people at the gate responded positively to this agreement and deal. They also blessed Boaz and Ruth saying, *"We are witnesses! May the Lord make the woman who is now coming into your home like Rachel and Leah, from whom all the nation of Israel descended! May you be great in Ephrathah and famous in Bethlehem.*

4 – MARRIAGE AND MOTHERHOOD

And may the Lord give you descendants by this young woman who will be like those of our ancestor Perez, the son of Tamar and Judah" (Ruth 4:11-12).

Boaz was a man who naturally blessed people by his words so it was not surprising that the people at the gate blessed him also in this new marriage with Ruth. Child of God, be careful, what goes round comes round. Little did Boaz know that by protecting Ruth from his workers, he was actually preserving her who by God's sovereign plan would later become his wife. How do you as a boss protect your female or male workers and subordinates? Can God trust you with the opposite sex who might be at a vulnerable stage in life? Do you take time to be interested in the pains and challenges of others? What provision do you have for the less fortunate at work?

Ruth was a woman of character. Character is the sum total of morals by which a person is judged, it is our integrity especially when others are not there. Ruth was committed to her mother-in-law and stood by her commitment. We must learn to stand by our commitment to the Lord and to each other. Ruth was committed to a new and different culture. In the same way, we as Christians ought to be committed to heaven's culture not our denomination's culture. Whereas heaven does not sanction homosexuality, lying or telling 'half truths', stealing, gossiping,sexual or physical abuse, laziness, racism, etc, many churches arecompromising on these issues. Ruth disciplined herself in the area of sexual relationships even though her husband had died and she was free to re-marry. Little did she envisage that she would become the wife of the multi-millionaire Boaz.

In the same place that she started begging for work, she would one day be the wife of the farm owner. It is not unusual that God's ordained means of blessing His children come in disguise or challenges. God's ways will always be mysterious in our eyes. He charts the paths of the seas and oceans, the path of the clouds in the sky, the path of the winds and the air, the path of all of His children. God rewarded Boaz, for through him and Ruth, Jesus Christ had His human roots: Boaz married Ruth and took her home to live with him. When he slept with her, the Lord enabled her to become pregnant, and she gave birth to a son (see verse 13).

There was rejoicing by the women of the city at the birth of Naomi's grandson: *They said, "Now at last Naomi has a son again!" And they named him Obed. He became the father of Jesse and the grandfather of David (verse 17).*

Ruth's coming to seek refuge in the God of Israel led to her being mentioned in the genealogy of Jesus Christ. She who was nobody became someone thereafter. She who was condemned by law and her background as a Moabite, crushed physically and emotionally because of her husband, father and brother-in-law's death, through God's grace was exalted in a foreign land.

God has all the earth in His Hands. He is never limited by anything, anywhere. He is able to make us blossom wherever we find ourselves. Child of God as we seek refuge in the God of Israel, He would make ways for us and make all things work together for our good in Jesus name. It is in God and through Him that the believer can be fruitful. Jesus Christ is our kinsman, redeemer, and restorer of all that we might have lost. He alone can nourish us all our days.

Child of God, please stay faithful to God, don't compromise for you never know what lies ahead. Adversity is not sent to destroy you but to cleanse you and develop you. May the Lord open your eyes to see His plans and help you to follow them. You and I may not know what part we have in pointing others to Christ just as Ruth was used to point us to Jesus.

DIVINE APPOINTMENT WILL BRING DIVINE GRACE, WHICH THEN BRINGSDIVINE DIRECTION WHICH LEADS TO DIVINE FAVOUR, WHICH IN TURN LEADS TO DIVINE BLESSINGS AND FINALLY DIVINE DESTINY.

May your divine appointment today with the Lord bring you into your divine destiny in Jesus' name. Please prayerfully consider this Psalm:

> *He that dwelleth in the secret place of the most High shall abide under the shadow of the Almighty.*
> *I will say of the LORD, He is my refuge and my fortress: my God; in him will I trust.*

Surely he shall deliver thee from the snare of the fowler, and from the noisome pestilence.

He shall cover thee with his feathers, and under his wings shalt thou trust: his truth shall be thy shield and buckler.

Thou shalt not be afraid for the terror by night; nor for the arrow that flieth by day;

Nor for the pestilence that walketh in darkness; nor for the destruction that wasteth at noonday.

A thousand shall fall at thy side, and ten thousand at thy right hand; but it shall not come nigh thee.

Only with thine eyes shalt thou behold and see the reward of the wicked.

Because thou hast made the LORD, which is my refuge, even the most High, thy habitation;

There shall no evil befall thee, neither shall any plague come nigh thy dwelling.

For he shall give his angels charge over thee, to keep thee in all thy ways.

They shall bear thee up in their hands, lest thou dash thy foot against a stone.

Thou shalt tread upon the lion and adder: the young lion and the dragon shalt thou trample under feet.

Because he hath set his love upon me, therefore will I deliver him: I will set him on high, because he hath known my name.

He shall call upon me, and I will answer him: I will be with him in trouble; I will deliver him, and honor him.

With long life will I satisfy him, and shew him my salvation. (Psalms 91: 1-16)

MY PERSONAL NOTES

EPILOGUE
THE EAGLE BIRD

Much has been written about the eagle bird — the king of the air — its size, strength, place of abode, hunting skills, etc. I will only want to concentrate on the training an eaglet receives from its parents comparing it with how God trains each one of His children.

Experts say that eaglets are hatched from 1 to 4 eggs laid by the parent eagle into a multilayer, wide, thick stick nest made by parents on a cliff or in tall trees. Each eaglet is fed with fresh animal flesh by the parents. Each eaglet's training exercise is determined by the parent and supervised by it. As the eaglets mature enough for them to learn to fly, mother eagle starts to disturb the nest by gradually removing many of the comfort materials that were there before.

This brings some discomfort to the eaglet and causes some concern for it. At the appropriate time for each eaglet, mother eagle drops it from the great height and watches as the eaglet begins to fall rapidly down, scared, perhaps screaming and trying out its wings, which up to this time have not been very much in use. Just before the eaglet crashes to the ground, mother eagle with its sharp eyesight sweeps down under the falling eaglet accurately, such that the eaglet lands on the mother's back and not on the ground. Mother eagle then carries the frightened eaglet back to the nest, and allows it to rest. The process is repeated over a period of time until the eaglet gets the message that is, to learn to exercise its wings, use them and not be frightened by heights or falling from a great height.

In the same way, when we first come to the Lord, He through the Holy Spirit feeds us with fresh food through His Word and answers our prayers often times before or while we are saying the prayers. When the Holy Spirit knows we are ready according to His individualised and custom-made training package, we may then experience a period of delayed or unanswered prayers that could be very frightening for any child of God. It is not uncommon for God to allow us to go through challenging times, painful, faith testing, faith building, faith exercising, and difficult, impending seemingly disgraceful circumstances knowing that this would lead us to recognise His provision and use our spiritual wings.

God's eyes are sharp, seeing through all things, at the same time, all the time, everywhere. His ears are open to all of His creation including even the sparrow in the fields. He comes accurately and swiftly bears us on His wings sometimes at a quarter to or a minute to disgrace or failure.' He shows up on time according to

His timetable not ours. The eagle never fears any storm; in fact it is happy with storms, as it uses it to soar higher in the sky. For those of us who have given our lives to Jesus Christ, any storm of life should be taken as a spring board to higher heights for we know **God makes all things to work for our good** as we love Him and are called according to His purpose (Romans 8:28).

Unlike the eaglet, for those who have given their lives to Christ, we remain God's children. We go through the school of God's training all through our lifetime as the Holy Spirit trains us and moulds Godly character and integrity in us. As we trustingly remain under His wings, we are guaranteed divine protection, warmth, provision and a personalised guided training. Our Good God is with us all the way!

POEMS

MORE ENCOURAGING THOUGHTS

DEATH

Death, death, death
Very common yet least talked about
Young people die and old people die too
Boys and girls die, men and women die too
Africans, Japanese, Caucasian, Jews all die
Common to all people from all background
Common to all tribes at all times of the day
Common all week, month and all year round.

Some die from sickness, others die without sickness
Some die from starvation, others die from overfeeding
Some die from poverty, others die in their wealth
Some die amidst their families, others without their families
Some die in war or battle, others die amidst great peace
Death ends it all for all people whenever it comes to them
Nothing can stop anyone born of a woman from physical death.

Doctors and nurses, patients and others good or bad die
Kings, queens, princes, princesses and peasants die
The wisest of the wise and the most stupid die too
The best intellectuals and the non-intellectuals die
The most successful and the non successful in life die
Single, married, separated or divorced people die too
Death is a common denominator says the Bible.

There is physical death and there is spiritual death
Physical death cuts you off from living here on earth
Spiritual death cuts you off from living there in heaven
Physical death cuts you off from your loved ones on earth
Spiritual death cuts you off from your own Creator
Physical death cannot be avoided by anyone
Spiritual death can be avoided by all who choose to
Only our Creator knows how each one will physically die.

Physical death is not the end of life as many people think
*Physical death is a result of our Adamic sin
**Spiritual death is a result of unbelief in Jesus Christ
Physical death is a passage to the continuation of life beyond
eternity of the soul of each person will be in heaven or hell
For those who have Jesus Christ as their Lord in heaven
For those who reject Jesus Christ as their Lord in hell
Settle the continuation of your life beyond now
as you choose or reject Jesus.

   * *Genesis 2:16-17, 3:1-19*
   ** *John 3:16-18, Romans 3:23, 6:23*
   © *O. Ola- Ojo. 19.02.03*

GOD HAS ANOTHER PLAN

When you lose your beloved one to sickness
Despite the best available medical care
And the loss is too much to bear
Be assured beloved, for God has another plan

When the illness seems to be tarrying for so long
And doctors have run short of medications to use
And the pains are becoming very much unbearable
Hang in there beloved, for God has another plan.

When you suddenly loose your precious job
And the bills are rolling in, in the usual envelopes
With no obvious new job in sight at the least
Don't give up beloved, for God has another plan.

When the creditors are on your back or at your tail
And you have not been able to meet your financial obligations
Due to no obvious fault of yours
Don't commit suicide beloved, for God has another plan.

When you fail that professional examination yet again
Despite your burning the midnight oil and working hard
With no courage to read let alone face another examination
Don't give up beloved, for God has another plan.

When your trusted spouse or business partner walks out on you
At the most inappropriate time and in an unpleasant manner
Children to look after or business deals to sort out all by yourself
Don't doubt in yourself, for God has another plan.

When you are not given that much wanted business contract
Despite your wonderful brief and excellent presentations
And the many hours and resources you have committed to it
Never give up beloved, for God has another plan.

God's plans are not near to any plans of ours
His plans for each of us His children
Are plans of good not of evil
To give us a future and bring us to an expected end.

His plans are way far from our plans
In the same way as His ways are far from ours
Like the sun and moon are far from us
Much more than we can hope for and beyond our imagination

In that present circumstance dearly beloved,

*God through Jesus Christ is waiting for you
Give all your loss and failed plans to the Lord
And watch Him unfold His wonderful plan for you.*
    © O. Ola Ojo. 22.10.02

I WILL LIFT UP MY EYES - PSALMS 121

I will lift up my eyes to the mountains; from whence shall my help come? verse 1.

Lord when I look at the mountains, they seem way high up above, solid, strong and immovable. My help however cannot come from the mountains as they are without life themselves.

My help comes from the Lord, who made heaven and earth. verse 2.

Lord in times past, my help has come from You, Maker of heaven and earth. Even though You are my Father and Lord by creative and redemptive rights, yet it seems You are so far away from me at the moment as my cries to You for help have not been answered. If You would help me, I know none of Your creatures can stand in my way of progress. Right now, I need Your help against my adversaries and oppressors who to me appear way high up like the mountains.

He will not allow my foot to slip, He who keeps me will not slumber. Behold He who keeps Israel will neither slumber nor sleep. verses 3-4.

Lord, these words express how vulnerable I am without Your help. These days I cannot feel You holding my hands and I fear that my foot is about to slip. Much as I believe that You do not sleep nor slumber to loose Your grip on me, yet I do not feel

Your hold as before and as a child I am frightened, and feel completely alone and abandoned.

The Lord is my keeper. The Lord is my shade on my right. The Sun will not smite me by day nor the moon by night. verses 5 -6.

Thank You Lord for being my keeper. You have been my protector in times past. Please come and once again be a shade for me from the surrounding heat of oppression, injustice, wickedness, poverty, failure, loss and loneliness so that I might not be smitten by them in Jesus name.

The Lord will protect me from all evil. He will keep my soul. verses 7.

Please Lord protect me according to Your promise from all forms of evil including unbelief and pride, which may want to attack my soul at this time of great need and keep my soul from denying You.

The Lord will guard my going in and coming out from this time forth and ever more. verse 8.

Thank You Lord for the promise of guarding my ways and being with me forever. As I daily go about my duties and tasks, may I experience Your leading and protection once more and always in Jesus name. (Amen.)
   © Ola-Ojo. 1995.

THE MORE DIFFICULT THE NEARER HE IS

The more difficult my situation
The nearer my Saviour is to me
The more weary and tired I feel
The more heavenly strength I am given

The more pains I have to bear
The greater the grace of God I experience
The more bitter the situation
The sweeter the joy of the Lord
The more foolish I am willing to be for His sake
The more of God's wisdom and knowledge I receive
The greater the trials and temptation
The stronger my faith becomes in Him
The more confusion and hopelessness around
The more of the Spirit's presence and direction for me
The more desperate the situation becomes
The nearer and bigger the awaiting miracle for me
The greater the threatening storm of life
The more of His peace that passes all understanding.
  © Ola-Ojo. 25/05/93

MEETING GOD IN ADVERSITY

Beloved when do you think that it's best to meet God?
You might say anytime and anywhere
You might likely say when the going is good
When there is peace, prosperity and success.

How easy to forget that God is always there
Especially in the face of real adversity
In the face of loss, uncertainty and fear
At the hour when it seems we can no longer cope.

Many great men and women in the past and present
Met God in the face of real pressure and problems
Many staking their very life for their faith in God
Many did die with no compromise on their belief

Meeting God in adversity could be very fruitful
Moses' meeting God in Midian in the burning bush
Was the turning point in his life
And the beginning of the deliverance of Israel from Egypt.

Daniel's encounter with God in the fierce lions' den
Led to the king's belief and declaration for God
It brought about the destruction of his persecutors
And great prosperity to Daniel thereafter.

For Shadrach, Meshach and Abednego in Babylon
In the flaming furnace they experienced the presence of God
They weren't hurt by the flames as expected
Enjoying the reality of God's abiding presence and protection.

Jonah's unique experience in the belly of the fish in the sea
For three days' submarine trip in the fish
In such adversity of possible death and uncertainty
He met God and was never the same again.

Jeremiah, shut up in a deep pit in the courtyard of a person
With no ability to get out of it or help himself
Received powerful words of God in that situation
The reality of God's comfort and presence he felt.

Paul's many writings to the Churches as recorded in the Bible
Were written in the prison cells cut off from brethren
Not only was he witnessing in each prison cell
He was writing reassuring, encouraging messages too.

Beloved when you find yourself in adversity
In the deep pit of hopelessness, loss or uncertainty
In the shackles of demonic yokes and bondage
Cheer up for even there God is able to meet you.

The unique experiences that follow God's allowed adversity
Bring comfort, reassurance and faith to God's child
And subsequent glory to the Almighty God Himself
Indeed working together for your good in the end.

You might today have to experience adversity
In the flaming furnace of hatred and ungodliness
In the threats of oppression and many attacks
In the wilderness of loneliness with no one to talk to.

Be it in the face of abject poverty with many possibilities
That of thirst, hunger, death or great need with no resource
Maybe that of heartless threats from the creditors
Be assured even there beloved that God is there with you.

Romans 8:28 & Jeremiah 33:2-3

© Ola-Ojo '92

THE TIDES

We live in a world which like the ocean surface is ripple full
What more with the very strong tides blowing periodically
On each one no matter the race, colour, sex, age or size
Sometimes very frightening are these tides even to the child of God.

The tide may be strong enough to capsize the boat of anyone
Leading to an unpredictable, expensive destruction and loss
Especially for an unbeliever who is like the house built on the sand.
This is different for a believer with strong anchor in the Lord.

For a child of God when the strong winds do come
Rather than capsizing our lifeboat and faith in God
We are lifted higher and closer to God the stronger the tide
What more making us better believing and practising Christians.

The strong tide of jealousy made Joseph's brothers sell him
To the Midian merchants who resold him to Portiphar in Egypt
The strong tide of adultery led to his indefinite imprisonment
Which in the end led to his becoming Egypt's Governor.

The yearly tide of taunting by Peninnah
Led the desperate barren Hannah to the tabernacle alone
Crying out her heart in silent words to the Almighty God
He gave her Samuel the prophet and five other children.

The incoming strong tide of death from Pharaoh the King
Led to Moses running to the land of Midian for forty years
There he got a wife, had two children and what more
Received God's personal commission to lead Israel out of Egypt.

The unquenchable tide of jealousy and impending death
Made David abandon his post at the palace of Saul
Running into and roaming in the wilderness for many years
Became his preparation as a king, poet and strong composer.

The callous and unsympathetic tide of the loan collector
Drove the widow to Prophet Elisha for help and counsel
Not only did she experience the miracle of the flowing olive oil
She paid her debt, secured her children and became prosperous.

The strong tide of ignorance and foolishness of the devil
Made the Pharisees crucify Jesus Christ on the cross
What was supposed to end His life, brought eternal life
To mankind of every generation and race who in Him will believe.

The strong tide of wickedness of the Jews of that time
Led to the many sufferings of Paul especially that of imprisonment
What a blessing in disguise as Paul's epistles were written
Whilst serving his prison sentence in chains in the jail.

Beloved today you too might be facing a strong tide
Which might seem overwhelming and life threatening
Cheer up, for underneath the strong tide of trials and tribulations
Lies the Sovereign God's triumph and unimaginable blessings.
   © *Ola - Ojo 07/08/92.*

THE UNFAILING SOURCE

Of man's basic needs, food and water are very important
Whilst some people can do without both for some days,
Others simply find it very difficult not to eat or drink.
However strong any man may be, he still needs to eat and drink.

Elijah the prophet was commanded by God to speak the word
There was not going to be rain in Israel for several years
What a big problem this would bring to the nation of Israel
In terms of their feeding and drinking, which would be affected.

Speaking the word did not exempt Elijah from the foreseen famine
How faithful the Almighty God was, for He had made provision
First Elijah was instructed by God to hide by Cherith brook
From where he could drink whilst ravens fed him.

God's channel of feeding Elijah with water, bread and meat
Was through the Cherith brook and faithful heavenly ravens
Alas after some time the brook dried up for there was no rain
And the brook had no water of it's own to offer Elijah the prophet.

Even when Elijah's channel of feeding and drinking dried up
And the brook was in no good state to help itself or Elijah
For the brook was merely a channel of blessing not the source
God still faithfully provided for Elijah throguh another channel.

God then commanded Elijah to go the village of Zarephath

Where he would meet a widow who will feed him from then
Obediently he arose and to Zarephath near Sodom City he went
Arriving just in time to see a widow gathering sticks.

Elijah first asked her for a cup of water to quench his thirst
Then he added the request for a bite of bread from the widow
What should have been the last meal for the widow and her son
Received God's blessing enough to feed them through the famine.

Dearly beloved, haven't we all worried at one time or the other
Concerning our basic needs especially regarding our feeding?
When your known channel of feeding dries up what do you do?
Don't run around, confused and worried on what next to do?

Beloved, when sometimes the channel of meeting your need dries up
Maybe because of the prevailing circumstances around you
Maybe because of the withdrawal of your job or business
Maybe because of reasons you cannot just know or understand.

Remember God has many more channels of blessings available
Which He is able to meet your needs with as you prayefully ask
The channel may dry up for whatever reason, dearly beloved
But God, the unfailing source will never dry up for your needs.

At such trying times when your basic needs are being threatened
And the channel you have been trusting fails you without notice
And the 'mountain gods' cannot help nor provide you help
Look up in faith to the Almighty God, the unfailing source.

*1kings 17: 1-16 and Psalm 121: 1-8

© *Ola-Ojo. 13/06/91*

OPPORTUNITY TO BECOME A CHRISTIAN

Dear FATHER IN HEAVEN,
Thank you for the privilege of reading this book. Indeed I have sinned and come short of Your glory. I am grateful to You for sending Jesus Christ into this world to come to die on the cross of Calvary for me. I believe in my heart that Jesus Christ paid for my sins, past, present and future. I believe Jesus Christ was buried and on the third day He rose from the dead. I believe that Jesus Christ will come back again . I confess with my mouth and I accept Him now to be my Lord, Master, Saviour, Brother, and Friend. I ask in Your mercy for the infilling of the Holy Spirit so that with His help, I can live a victorious life becoming all that You have ordained me to be in Jesus' name I pray with thanksgiving. Amen.

If after reading this book you said the above prayer and became born-again, please fill out the tear-off slip below and send to the address as shown.

The booklet, *Congratulations! You are born again* is for those who have done so through reading this book. It is a free booklet that we would like to send to you.

In it the frequently asked questions are answered and this will get you on the way to growing in your newfound faith in God. You can also download this free booklet from our website: www.protokospublishers.com

You are also free to contact any of the organisations listed at the end of the book.

I look forward to hearing from you soon.

O. Ola-Ojo (2008)

REQUEST SLIP
(TEAR OFF OR MAKE A COPY OF THIS SLIP)
Please fill out this slip and mail the address below:

_____

To receive your free booklet, **Congratulations! You Are Born Again**, simply fill in this slip with all the details requested and send to the address at the end of the slip:

Title:_____

First name:_____

Surname:_____

Address:_____

_____

Zip/PostCode: _____ Country: _____

Email: _____

Phone *(day)*: _____ *(evening)*: _____
(Please include country & area code)

Best time to call *(pls tick)*: ❏ day   ❏ evening   ❏ anytime.

Any urgent prayer request(s)? *(Please, use extra sheets if required)*:

_____

_____

_____

_____

_____

Protokos Publishers
P. O. Box 48424, London, SE15 2YL, UK

+44 (0) 7534831807 I www.protokospublishers.com
info@protokospublishers.com I protokospublishers@yahoo.co.uk

TEAR OFF HERE

BOOKS BY THE AUTHOR

Provocation, Prayer and Praise
(December 2004)

Complimentary to The Christian and Infertility this book focuses on the story of an infertile woman in the Bible, her provocations, prayer and praise. Whatever makes you incomplete, unfulfilled, less than whom God made you to be, whatever issue of life that the enemy uses to provoke you calls for prayer.

Key features:
- Some known medical reasons for infertility in the woman
- Why Hannah went to the house of God in spite of her barrenness
- Is it true that the husband is much more than 10 sons to the infertile woman?
- When, where and how to address the source/cause of your provocation
- God's part and your part in that promise
- God is able to meet that humanly impossible need of yours
- A time to celebrate and praise God

Book Details:
- Paperback: 62 pages
- Language English
- ISBN-10: 1412026903
- ISBN-13: 978-1412026901
- www.protokospublishers.com

A Reader from London
7 Jan 2006 on Amazon.co.uk
An excellent easy to read and understand book. The principles shared in this book though primarily are for those trying for a baby could as well be applied to any area of hurt and unfulfilment.

The Christian and Infertility
(December 2004)

The Christian and Infertility addresses one of the often neglected needs of Christian couples. It gives an insight into infertility from the biblical and medical perspectives. It is written not only for potential fruitful couples but for pastors, family and friends of these couples. It is written that the Body of Christ might be fully equipped to know and support couples who are facing the challenge of infertility at present.

Key features:
- Childlessness in the Bible and lessons to learn;
- Some possible physical, medical and environmental causes of infertility;
- Some known spiritual causes of infertility;
- Some of the available treatment options in the UK;
- Choices of fertility treatment;
- Should a Christian professional be involved in fertility treatment?

Book Details:
- Paperback: 150 pages
- Language English
- ISBN-10: 1412026911
- ISBN-13: 978-1412026918
- www.protokospublishers.com

A reviewer from Glen Burnie, MD, USA
29 Oct 2007 on Amazon.co.uk
This book is a great eye-opener for all. It sheds light on infertility from the medical and spiritual angle and gives the reader a balance as I believe every human being is made up of both physical and spiritual part. For balance in life, the two parts must be well fed. One cannot concentrate on the spiritual and neglect the physical. This book which is quite inspiring also reminds us that God has a way of sorting us out... I will recommend it to everybody trusting God for any form of blessing to get one and apply it to their situation. It will definitely bless you and yours.

Obstetrics and Gynaecology Ultrasound - A Self-Assessment Guide

June 2005, Churchill Elsevier Publishers, UK

This self-assessment guide is a structured questions and answer book that develops the reader's understanding capability using a simple method in treating related topics. Clinical indications are presented with their corresponding ultrasound findings using appropriate illustrations. A case study approach is followed; presenting the clinical and ethical dilemmas that might arise whilst encouraging students to think. The aim is to reinforce theoretical knowledge within a clinical environment.

Key features:
- Over 600 high-resolution ultrasound images
- Covers a wide spectrum of ultrasound curriculum
- Includes a detailed study of fertility
- Aids quick understanding of the subject matter

Book Details:
- 468 pages
- ISBN-10: 0443064628
- ISBN-13: 978-0443064623
- Book Dimensions: 24 x 16.8 x 2.6 cm
- www.protokospublishers.com

"...This excellent new book is a study guide... This is an attractive paperback that should be essential reading for trainee obstetric and gynaecological sonographers, whether they are radiographers or radiology or obstetric trainees. It will be of particular value to those preparing for the RCOG/RCR Diploma in Advanced Obstetric Ultrasound and to specialist registrars in obstetrics and gynaecology undertaking special skills modules in fetal medicine, gynaecological ultrasound and infertility..."

Reviewer: Ann Harper, MD, FRCPI, FRCOG
Consultant Obstetrician & Gynaecologist,
Royal Jubilee Maternity Service, Belfast, UK
The Obstetrician & Gynaecologist,
www.rcog.org.uk/togonline Book reviews 2006

Good Mums, Bad Mums
(June 2005)

This is in two parts, the main chapter that can be used for personal or group study, and an accompanying exercise section. The privileged position of a mother is in her being a co-creator with God and bringing forth life (lives). This book compliments one of God's previous revelations to me as contained in the book titled Good Dads, Bad Dads'. Whilst the father could be likened to the pilot of the family plane, the mother can be likened to the force behind the plane –positive or negative. Good mothers are not only co-creators with God, they also do nurture as well as nourish their children physically, emotionally and spiritually.

Keys features:
- Were all the mothers in the Bible good mothers?
- Lessons from the strengths and weaknesses of seven mothers
- Be encouraged – you are not alone in the assignment of motherhood
- Be motivated in the areas of your strengths
- Learn ways of supporting your husband and children

Book Details:
- Paperback: 160 pages
- Language: English
- ISBN-10: 1597813486
- ISBN-13: 978-1597813488
- Book Dimensions: 21.4 x 14 x 1.4 cm
- www.protokospublishers.com

To The Bride With Love
(2007)

Every wise woman preparing to get married knows she will need sound advice, practical tips and solid, heartfelt prayers, of those who have travelled on the road she is about to journey on. In this book, 10 women of different age groups, from different backgrounds and cultures who wedded under various circumstances, individually share their experience with the bride in an intimate, very candid and unforgettable way.

Keys features:
- To the Bride with Love is the perfect bride's evergreen companion. The content is suitable, relevant and applicable even decades after the wedding day.
- To the Bride with Love is an ideal wedding gift on its own. It can also accompany any other gift (big or small) that you have for the bride but take this hint... the bride will keep thanking you for the book years and years after.

Book details:
- Paperback: 108 pages
- Language: English
- ISBN-10: 1434302520
- ISBN-13: 978-1434302526
- Book dimensions: 22.4 cm x 15 cm x 1 cm
- www.protokospublishers.com

One of the best, 19 Jul 2008 Amazon.com
Sade Olaoye "clare4good" (UK)
This book has really helped my marriage from the onset as I got it as a wedding gift, God bless the giver. It's a must read for relationship improvement and Gods' guidance. I recommend people to get for oneself and also as a great blessing for someone else in love.

Review by Oyinlola Odunlami
Shallom Bookshop, SE London UK
The style of this book reminds me of Francine Rivers, one of the best

authors in Christian novels in the USA, whose style is so engrossing that you can't put her books down until you read the end of the story.

Nevertheless, the writing style of Oluwakemi is unique, peculiar and distinct to herself. I recommend To the Bride with Love to wives, wives to be, mothers, mentors, youth leaders and workers. Why? The clarity, the focus and the intent of this book is so empowering, encouraging and enlightening that it will definitely mould or re mould a life to achieve its purpose. The truth is, there are very few books that have depth as well as help you to achieve your goals and arrive at your destination. Many books tend to excite you but have no depth; you read and you forget; they do not really change you but this book, To the Bride with Love will definitely leave a word in your spirit and move you to your next level!

I believe that this is also a book that pastors will find useful as a manual for marriage counseling, because many books on marriage focus mostly on what you as an individual can gain, your own personal satisfaction while little is said about the sacrifices involved and their importance. As my pastor usually says, it is important to learn from those who have gone ahead, understand why some were successful and others weren't, so that we won't fall where they fell, rather, we would gain more speed, achieve our goals and thereby glorify Christ.

So, I invite you not only to get a copy of this life-changing manual for yourself, but also to put it into as many hands as you can afford to, for then the world will definitely benefit and your life will be a blessing to many.

COMING OUT SOON!!

Grace or Works?

This book makes you examine a lot of issues in your life, family relationships in particular, that you may have taken for granted or totally ignored. As conveyed right from the rhetorical question posed in the title, Grace or Works, the author stirs you towards asking yourself pertinent questions, thinking through for answers and even getting solutions for unresolved problems.

Have you heard of prodigal wives, husbands, mothers or prodigal fathers? This book identifies and defines them clearly. For anyone experiencing a crises in their relationship with such prodigal family members, this book, which is based on the parable of the "Prodigal son" in Luke 15:11-32 is a one-stop resource material to meet your counselling needs. And just in case you happen to be the prodigal who has caused your relatives much sorrow, there is hope for you in this book.

Interspersed with prayers for you by the author and specific prayers that you can say for yourself, as well as poems to comfort and inspire you, Grace or Works not only asks you questions, it helps you make and maintain the right choices.

Key features include:
- The younger son's request
- His trip to a far country
- His relationships away from home
- The investment of his inheritance
- His lowest and turning point
- His open repentance and confession to his father
- His big brother's attitude
- Their father's response to both of them

Book detail(s):
- Paperback
- Language: English
- ISBN: 978-0-9557898-5-4

USEFUL LINKS & ADDRESSES:

Aglow International
Website: www.aglow.org

Aglow International is a network of caring women, a faith-building organisation rooted in local groups and international in scope, yet one-on-one in ministry. Their mission is to lead women to Jesus Christ and provide opportunity for Christian women to grow in their faith and minister to others.

Care for the Family
P. O. Box 488
Cardiff, CF15 7YY
United Kingdom

Tel: (029) 2081 0800
Fax: (029) 2081 4089
Email: mail@cff.org.uk
Website: www.care-for-the-family.org.uk OR www.cff.org.uk

Care for the Family aims to promote strong family life and to help those hurting because of family breakdown. Their heart is to come alongside people in the good times and in the tough times—bringing hope, compassion and some practical, down-to-earth help and encouragement.

Children Evangelism Ministry, Inc.
P. O. Box 4480
Ilorin, Kwara State, Nigeria

Tel: +234 31 222199
Email: cem562000@yahoo.com

Children Evangelism Ministry Inc., is a Ministry that reaches out with the Gospel to Children before and after birth. The ministry teaches and equips parents, teachers and coordinators of Sunday School and children's clubs. They also have and hold children's clubs, conferences and training seminars.

Focus on the Family
Tel: 1-800-232-6459
Website: www.family.org

Focus on the Family cooperate with the Holy Spirit in disseminating the Gospel of Jesus Christ to as many people as possible, and, specifically, to accomplish that objective by helping to preserve traditional values and the institution of the family.

Radio Bible Class (RBC) Ministries

P. O. Box 1
Camforth, Lancashire
LA5 9ES
United Kingdom

Among other forms of spreading the Gospel, RBC prints Our Daily Bread, a free daily devotional reading available for residents in the UK and Republic of Ireland.

The Shepherd's Ministries

5 Brookehowse Road
Bellingham
London
SE6 3TJ
United Kingdom
Tel/Fax: +44 208 698 7222

Email: info@theshepherdsministries.org
Website: www.theshepherdsministries.org

The Shepherd's Ministries helps to bring Children into an experience of worshipping God in truth and in spirit; gives children a world-view based on God's word and mission and helps children to exercise their gifts in local and global missions.

United Christian Broadcasting UCB

P. O. Box 255, Stoke on Trent, ST4 8YY, United Kingdom
Tel: +44 1782 642 000
Fax: +44 1782 641 121
Email: ucb@ucb.co.uk
Website: www.ucb.co.uk

Among other forms of spreading the Gospel, UCB prints The Word For Today, a free daily devotional reading available for residents in the UK and Republic of Ireland.

www.ingramcontent.com/pod-product-compliance
Lightning Source LLC
Chambersburg PA
CBHW051452290426
44109CB00016B/1731